P9-ARJ-806

HEROES IN GREEK MYTHOLOGY ROCK!

Karen Bornemann Spies

E **Enslow Publishers, Inc.**
40 Industrial Road
Box 398
Berkeley Heights, NJ 07922
USA

http://www.enslow.com

To Carolynn,
with thanks for your encouragement and assistance.

Original edition published as *Heroes in Greek Mythology* in 2002

Library of Congress Cataloging-in-Publication Data

Spies, Karen Bornemann.
    Heroes in Greek Mythology Rock! / Karen Bornemann Spies.
        p. cm. — (Mythology rocks!)
    Includes bibliographical references and index.
    Summary: "Read about Perseus and Medusa, Jason and the Argonauts, Theseus and the Minotaur, and four other important Greek myths"—Provided by publisher.
    ISBN 978-0-7660-3900-1
    1. Mythology, Greek—Juvenile literature.   I. Title.
    BL785.S68 2012
    398.20938—dc22
    2010053431

Paperback ISBN: 978-1-59845-331-7

Printed in China

052011 Leo Paper Group, Heshan City, Guangdong, China.

10 9 8 7 6 5 4 3 2 1

To Our Readers: We have done our best to make sure all Internet addresses in this book were active and appropriate when we went to press. However, the author and the publisher have no control over and assume no liability for the material available on those Internet sites or on other Web sites they may link to. Any comments or suggestions can be sent by e-mail to comments@enslow.com or to the address on the back cover.

Cover and illustrations by William Sauts Bock

Contents

EUROPE
Mt. Olympus
Th
Adriatic Sea
Rome
Italy
Pillars of Heracles
Mediterranean Sea
Sicily
Ionian Sea
GREECE
Thessaly
Boeotia
Attica
Aegea
PELOPONNESUS
Thebes
Olympia
Corinth
Mycenae
Argos
Athens
Sparta
Aetolia
Thebes
ATTICA
Gulf of Corinth
ELIS
Mt. Erymanthus
Arcadia
Isthmus
Marathon
Athens
Mycenae
Argolia
Argive
Alpheus R.
Olympia
PELOPONNESUS
Corinth
Argos
Sparta
Medi
LIBYA
AFRICA
AF

Colchis ➝

Black Sea

Bosporus

Greek vase
painting of
grape picker

⊙Troy

Propontis
(Sea of Marmara)

Asia Minor

...Greek vase
painting of
olive picker

Sea

ace

Cnossus

CYPRUS

Middle East

erranean Sea

R   I EGYPT C   A

Nile R.

Preface

Our word *myth* comes from the ancient Greek word *mythos*, meaning "speech," "tale," or "story."[1] A myth is a traditional story that has been passed down from generation to generation. Early myths were passed down orally. Later, after a culture developed a system of writing, the myths were preserved on papyrus, an early form of paper, or inscribed on stones, walls, and other structures. Over the years, many myths have been collected and written down.

Although Greek mythology has existed for three thousand years, these ancient stories continue to fascinate people of all ages, mainly because they describe actions, problems, and feelings that are common to all human beings. Each of us has probably experienced anger, jealousy, joy, fear, and frustration, all of which are emotions common to the characters in Greek myths. We can imagine ourselves in many of the situations which the mortals in mythology faced or taking part in the exciting adventures and dangerous situations that challenged the Greek heroes.

Myths served several purposes for the ancient Greeks. First, they provided explanations for natural occurrences, such as thunder or the rising and setting of the sun. Secondly, they told stories about the origins of Greek customs and traditions. And, of course, myths provided entertainment—a relief from their busy and sometimes tedious lives.

Geography

The geography of Greece has always played an important role in the development of its people and its myths. The country of Greece is located on the European continent east of Italy on the Mediterranean Sea. It is surrounded by many islands, both large and small, including the island of Crete, the largest island in the Aegean. In the northern part of the mainland is the broad plain of Thessaly, where the city of Iolcus was located. South of this region is the plain of Boeotia, the location of the important city of Thebes. Greece also includes the Peloponnesus, a southern peninsula connected to the mainland by an isthmus near the ancient city of Corinth. The important cities of Sparta, Olympia, Tiryns, Mycenae, and Argos were located on the Peloponnesus. The city of Athens is located on the southern tip of the mainland in a region known as Attica.

Greece is blessed with sunny skies and generally mild winters. Hills and mountains dominate the landscape, and between the mountain ranges lie the plains, which are the only location suitable for farming. Still, the mountainous soil is dry and rocky, so farming is difficult. Grains, such as wheat and barley, and fruits and vegetables, such as grapes and olives, have been common crops throughout Greece's history. However, because of the difficulty of farming, the Greeks have consistently depended on the sea.

Thousands of years ago, the Greeks were already known as great seafarers who sailed all over the Mediterranean. Because of their widespread voyages, they came into contact with people from many different cultures. They traded goods with people in Asia Minor, Africa, Europe, and the Middle East. Each time the sailors met with people from different backgrounds, they eagerly listened to the stories these people told and added them to their already rich collection of myths. The widespread travel of the early Greeks helps to explain the different versions of each myth and why the myths of many different cultures often seem very similar.

History

Archaeological evidence shows that the earliest peoples settled on the Greek mainland prior to 70,000 B.C.; however, few specific details are known about the region until approximately 3000 B.C. Archaeologists have discovered bronze tools from this period that were used for farming and herding animals. The people lived in small villages that were often surrounded by thick walls.

In about 2000 B.C., tribes from the east came across Asia and settled in mainland Greece. They, too, built fortified towns and lived as farmers. At the same time, a powerful civilization developed on Crete. These people were known as the Minoans, after their king, Minos. The Minoans developed a powerful seagoing empire. They traded with cities on the other islands in the Aegean Sea, as well as with Sicily, Egypt, and cities on the eastern coast of the Mediterranean. The Minoan culture, known for its fabulous wealth, had a great influence on the art, religion, and culture of the Greek mainland.

The Mycenaean Age (1600 B.C.–1200 B.C.)

In about 1600 B.C., civilization on mainland Greece grew in power. The Greeks of this period are known as the Mycenaeans, after the city of Mycenae. They spoke a language that is similar to modern Greek. The Mycenaeans used a form of writing known as Linear B. It was used for keeping accounts, not for writing literature. Thus, myths during this period were still passed on by word of mouth. The Mycenaeans lived in independent kingdoms ruled by rich and powerful kings. They were fierce warriors who used bronze weapons and drove into battle in horse-drawn chariots. They built strong walls around their cities, for they were often at war with each other. Most of the major Greek myths are connected with Mycenaean cities and heroes.[2]

At about the same time that Mycenaean civilization blossomed, Minoan culture declined. Then, in about 1450 to 1400 B.C., the palaces on Crete were destroyed. Historians are not sure what caused the ruins. Archaeological evidence shows there were signs of fire and massive destruction. An earthquake may have struck the island. The Mycenaeans may have invaded and destroyed the island civilization. In any case, Minoan art and religious beliefs had a profound effect on the Greeks. These beliefs developed into stories about nature, animals, and gods with human forms. During Mycenaean times, some of these stories were blended into Greek myths such as the birth of Zeus, king of the gods, on Crete.

As their civilization spread, the Greeks lived in towns that were independent of each other. The people who lived in what is known today as Greece were united by two factors: They spoke roughly the same language, and they thought of themselves as "Hellenes," or fellow descendants of Hellen, the legendary founder of the Greek people. (Today the modern Greek word for the country of Greece is *Hellas*.) There was no single ruler and communities often warred against each other. It is vital to keep in mind that the people we call Greeks today were, at one time, not unified at all.

The Dark Age (1200 B.C.–800 B.C.)

In the eleventh century B.C., an unknown enemy destroyed the ancient city of Troy, located in the western part of Asia Minor. It was against this city that the Greeks supposedly fought as a single group in order to rescue Helen, the wife of Menelaus, the king of Sparta. The power of the Mycenaeans ended not long after the destruction of Troy in about 1250 B.C. The Mycenaean civilization probably began its decline because of continuing battles between the ancient Greek cities. However, historians believe that the final, widespread destruction came at the hands of the Dorians, a group of Greek-speaking invaders from the north and east.

The decline of Mycenaean culture ushered in a period in Greek history known as the Dark Age. Linear B writing disappeared. Extensive migration occurred far beyond the boundaries of present-day Greece. By this time, ancient Greece extended over a large area along the Mediterranean coasts and islands. Greek cities were established in Sicily and Italy. The powerful kings of Mycenaean civilization had given way to a society organized around the family and village life.

The Archaic Period (800 B.C.–475 B.C.)

In about 800 B.C., the Greeks developed their alphabet. They began to write down poems and plays as well as most of the stories that are now considered part of Greek mythology. A time of extensive cultural revival occurred. At this time, the various communities began to think of themselves as living in separate political entities known as city-states. The Greek word for city-state is *polis*. Each city-state was an independent, self-governing community that usually included the city and the surrounding rural area. Athens and Sparta were the most important city-states.

In 508 B.C., Athens became the first democracy in the world when adult free males were allowed to vote on issues related to governing the city. Democracy comes from the Greek words *demos*, "the people," and *kratein*, "to rule." However, only citizens could vote in this democracy and not everyone living in Athens was considered a citizen. Slaves and women were not considered citizens, and therefore, were not allowed to vote.

The Classical Period (About 500 B.C.–338 B.C.)

Athens soon became the center of important developments in Greek civilization. Under the leadership of the states-man Pericles, this period became known as the Golden Age of Pericles. Athenians achieved great accomplishments in philosophy, art, literature, history, and medicine, as well as government. Greek mythology reached a high point. The works of the Greek poet Homer, in particular, became the foundation of Greek education. Other city-states such as Sparta became jealous of Athens' power. In 431 B.C., the Peloponnesian War broke out between Sparta and Athens. Athens ultimately lost the war in 404 B.C., and the power of Athens declined.

The Hellenistic Age (4th century B.C.–1st century B.C.)

The Greeks continued to battle among themselves until 338 B.C., when Philip of Macedonia conquered most of the Greek mainland. (Macedonia is a region in the northern part of Greece.) After Philip's death, his son, Alexander, conquered additional territory. Alexander's reign extended over Asia Minor and Egypt all the way to India. It provided a unified government for all this territory, including Greece. However, Alexander died suddenly at the age of thirty-three, and his generals divided up his empire. Even though Greece was no longer politically unified, its cultural influence continued. Greek was the language spoken at this time. What is known as Greek, or Hellenistic influence continued for another thousand years or so.

In the meantime, the power of Rome was building as the Romans conquered many tribes in Italy. By about 150 B.C., Greece was completely under Roman control. The Romans demonstrated their respect for Greek culture by adopting many of its aspects. Although the Romans changed the names of many of the Greek gods, they kept most Greek myths intact.

Religion and Culture

The ancient Greeks were *polytheistic,* meaning they believed in many gods and goddesses. Their group, or collection, of gods and goddesses is called a *pantheon*, and the leader of the Greek pantheon was Zeus, the king of the gods. The ancient Greeks believed that the gods controlled nature and all events taking place on Earth. These gods were in the shape of human beings and felt human emotions such as anger, joy, and jealousy. They did not love human beings, and did not require humans to love them in return. They did, however, expect to be honored and respected, but they sometimes chose to act in ways that mortals disliked. In short, the Greek gods could act however they wished.

The gods were a major part of everyday life in ancient Greece, and each god controlled at least one aspect of human life. Zeus, for instance, was the ruler of the sky and the leader of the gods, but he was also a protector of guests and travelers.

Hera, Zeus' wife, was the goddess of marriage and childbirth. The Greeks believed that Pan, the god of forests and wildlife, protected shepherds. They thought that Athena, the goddess of wisdom and war, provided intelligence and courage.

The Greeks did not believe that the gods revealed their will in writing. Therefore, the priests for each god had no writings to interpret, so their function became one of performing ritual sacrifices in honor of that god. These sacrifices might take the form of killing an animal or the burning of special, sacred foods. Although human sacrifice was mentioned in a few myths, the actual performance of human sacrifice in the Greek culture was rare.

Most cities had a particular god or goddess whom they considered their special protector. Athens, for example, was named after its protector, Athena, goddess of wisdom and war. Athens considered Poseidon, god of the sea, to be another of its special protectors. Sacrifices to these gods were placed outside the god's temple on an altar.

The Greeks also believed in oracles, or prophets. At the temples of various gods, the priests, who could be either men or women, were often called upon to interpret omens, such as the sighting of a certain kind of bird or the appearance of some other natural event. The word *oracle* also refers to the prophecies that the priest gave. One of the most famous oracles was located at Delphi, where there were many important temples. People would travel from all over the Greek world in order to visit the temples and honor the gods. Apollo's oracle at Delphi was one of the most famous. This site can still be visited today.

The Greeks believed that the gods lived on Mount Olympus, a real mountain in the north central part of Greece called Thessaly. However, according to Greek tradition, the gods could leave Olympus and travel anywhere. Myths and legends often told of the gods taking on human forms and interacting with the people. Gods, Zeus in particular, often had children with mortal women. Less frequently, goddesses had romantic relationships with mortal men.

Within the pantheon, the gods often married each other, and some of them had more than one spouse or partner at a time. Sometimes the gods married their siblings, parents, or children. The god Zeus, for example, had many partners other than his wife, Hera, who was also his sister. The gods and goddesses were often paired in different ways because the myths were always developing and being retold. Zeus, as the king of the gods and the most powerful god, often seemed to be a part of all the other gods' lives.

Although the gods had affairs and children with many different partners, actual Greek marriage customs were very strict. Women were married at a young age, usually in their teens, to men who were much older; and the marriages, at least in Athens, were usually arranged by families based on economic needs and political tactics, rather than affection. It was not socially acceptable for women to have relationships with men outside of marriage, regardless of what the gods and goddesses were thought to do.

Literature and Drama

The Greek myths we are familiar with today are the result of generations of storytelling. Many of the Greek myths we know are adaptations of stories that the Greeks gleaned from other cultures. It was via oral storytelling that myths and legends traveled from one part of Greece to another, as well as to other parts of the world. However, after 800 B.C., stories began to be written down, including most of the tales that we now recognize as the basic part of Greek mythology.

Sometime in the eighth century B.C., the poet Homer is thought to have composed the *Iliad* and the *Odyssey*. Homer has always been considered to be the author of both poems, although no historical proof of his authorship exists. The *Iliad* recounts the story of the tenth year of the Trojan War, which may actually have taken place around 1250 B.C., when the city of Troy was destroyed. The *Odyssey* tells the story of the adventures of Odysseus, a legendary ruler from the real island of Ithaca, located off the west coast of the Greek mainland. Legend has it that Homer was born in the eighth century B.C. on Chios, an island in eastern Greece, or in Smyrna, a seaport in what is now western Turkey. Because oral storytelling was such an important tradition before the advent of writing, Homer's stories may have been told for generations before they were ever written down.

Another important writer at this time was a poet known as Hesiod, who was born about 700 B.C. His two surviving poems are the *Theogony*, which tells the story of the mythic creation of the world, and *Works and Days*, which tells other important stories. These two works give us much information about the myths surrounding the various gods and goddesses in Greek legend and religion at this time.

During the time when democracy was developing in Athens, literature and the arts thrived. Theater was one of these arts. Athens' greatest playwrights were Aeschylus, Sophocles, and Euripides. Many of the myths about heroes that we know today are taken from their plays. Hero tales were especially suited to the medium of drama, because they include plots full of adventure and characters whose emotions, such as jealousy, vengefulness, and anger, were displayed at peak levels. Similar elements of suspense, violence, and tragedy continue to attract today's viewers of these dramas.

During the Hellenistic Age, the intellectual center of the Greek world was Alexandria, an Egyptian city with a library that was an influential site of Greek scholarship. Poets writing at this time included Apollonius of Rhodes and Theocritus of Cos. The *Argonautika* of Apollonius is the single most important source on the myth of Jason and the Argonauts. Poems of Theocritus included tales about Heracles as well as the Argonauts.

Another important source of Greek mythology actually comes from the Romans. When they conquered the Greeks, the Romans absorbed many aspects of the Greek culture. The poet Ovid, who lived from about 43 B.C. to A.D. 17, was an influential figure in Rome and a prolific writer. One of his most significant contributions to modern scholarship is his fifteen-volume work called *The Metamorphoses*, which retells the stories of many Greek myths.

After the invention of the Greek alphabet in the ninth century B.C., many Greek myths were copied by hand onto rolls of papyrus, an early form of paper. In the second to fifth centuries A.D., parchment pages bound into books replaced the papyrus rolls. For the next one thousand years after that, myths were copied onto vellum, a fine-grained animal skin, or onto paper. The first printed edition of a Homeric poem appeared in 1488.[3] It used a form of type that looked like Greek handwriting.

Another source of knowledge about Greek myths is archaeology, the study of ancient cultures. Paintings, statues, vases, and other nonliterary sources uncovered by archaeologists provide information about the people who created and listened to myths. A vase itself is not a myth; however, the illustrations inscribed on it can provide information about a character or a scene from a myth.

Hero Myths, or Legends

The myths in this book are legends, or myths about heroes. Heroes usually had a divine ancestor, such as a grandparent, or were born of a mortal and a god, although they were not considered divine. They were kings and queens, princes and princesses, and other members of nobility. Also, they were stronger and more physically attractive than ordinary mortals. In earlier times, heroes were not worshipped; however, as Greece emerged from the Dark Age, hero cults, a system of religious beliefs and practices in honor of a particular hero, developed.[4] Heroes were worshipped at shrines built in their honor at the location where they had supposedly died or been buried. Honoring a hero could bring good fortune, while neglecting the worship of a hero might incite the hero's displeasure. The development of the city-state brought an increase in hero worship.[5] Many city-states considered a particular hero to be their founder, and many cities or regions developed local heroes, such as Meleager at Calydon (see Chapter 3) and Theseus at Athens (see Chapter 7). Most Greeks believed that heroes had actually existed, and the members of many important families felt that they had descended from these noble ancestors.[6] The ancient Greeks believed that events that took place in these legends happened in the distant past, when heroes and heroines performed great feats and experienced fantastic adventures.

Scholars today believe that with each retelling of a legend, the storyteller made additions to make the myth more exciting. However, historians now feel that many Greek legends contain some factual elements about major events and political relationships that have been verified through archaeological discoveries. Many of the characters in hero myths probably lived during the Mycenaean times (1600–1200 B.C.).[7] Archaeologists have uncovered ruins of important locations described in legends, such as the palace of King Minos on the island of Crete and the maze in which he kept the Minotaur, a half-man, half-bull monster. Yet, although the lives of some of the heroes, such as Heracles, are thought to have some actual basis in fact and some real events may be described in myths, these tales should not be interpreted as pure history.

As each storyteller added his own details and embellishments, the legends about heroes lost their unadulterated historical basis. Instead, storytellers added elements of the folktale, a type of traditional tale like the fairy tales *Cinderella* or *Snow White*. Folktales, whose main purpose is to entertain, are often tales of adventure that feature fantastic beings. They commonly include certain elements, such as a dragon that guards a special object or a magical potion that protects against danger. The hero may be rewarded with the hand of the princess in marriage, or he may win the throne of a kingdom. A quest for a special object is a common theme of folktales and is a vital part of Greek hero tales.

The Greeks treasured hero myths because they described the character traits that the Greeks valued in their heroes, such as bravery in battle and an almost excessive striving for glory. A hero also had to remain true to his comrades in battle. In peacetime, a hero was expected to be honorable and loyal and show devotion to his family. A hero always offered hospitality to a guest. However, the tales of the heroes also described occasions when some of them acted in a manner that was unheroic. The hero might break a vow of friendship or marriage. He might even commit murder. However, as the myth unfolded, the hero typically atoned for his unheroic deed with feats of greater bravery.

Heroes of Greek myths had many characteristics in common.[8] Each hero had something mysterious or unusual about his conception or birth. Also, one parent was a god or a member of royalty. For example, the father of Perseus, a famous Greek hero whose story is told in Chapter 1, was Zeus, the king of the gods. Even when a hero had a parent that was a god, he still had a human nature. The hero felt joy and anger, fear and excitement. Commonly, the hero showed excessive pride, or *hubris*. Often, the hero believed in the power of fate— that the course of his life was already set. Fate plays an important role in the life and death of the hero Meleager, whose story is told in Chapter 3, "The Calydonian Boar Hunt."

A hero went on a journey or followed a quest toward a goal. He performed noble or dangerous tasks and faced loneliness.

Somehow, he resisted weaknesses that would have overcome ordinary humans. In the process of his quest, a hero might have to solve a riddle. For example, Theseus in Chapter 7, "Theseus and the Minotaur," had to find his way out of a maze. His solution of the puzzle could be compared to solving life's challenges.

Often, a hero might have a guide or receive some other kind of assistance. This assistance might be human or divine. It might take the form of a weapon or necessary information to finish the quest. For example, in Chapter 1, "Perseus and the Gorgon Medusa," two of the gods, Hermes, the divine messenger, and Athena, goddess of wisdom and war, helped Perseus to kill Medusa, a snake-headed monster. They gave him a sword and other gifts to help him on his quest.

Sometimes, the gods interfered in the quest in a negative way. Hera, queen of the gods and wife of Zeus, disliked Heracles, the greatest Greek hero, because he was the product of one of Zeus' many love affairs. Hera took out her anger on Heracles by causing him to go temporarily insane. This story is told in Chapter 5, "The Labors of Heracles."

Sometimes, part of the hero's quest required him to descend to the Underworld, which was ruled by the god Hades. This was where the Greeks believed the spirits of the dead lived. Sometimes the hero's journey was not an actual physical trip. Instead, it was an emotional journey, in which he faced his worst fears and loneliness. This descent, either physical or emotional, was the final test for the hero. He faced and conquered "death." In the process, he changed in some important way. For the last of his twelve labors, Heracles visited the Underworld. He learned courage in facing the powers of death as represented by Hades, god of the Underworld, and his hound, Cerberus. Heracles ultimately overcame death in the myth retold in Chapter 6, "The Lernaean Hydra and the Death of Heracles."

Greek heroes were almost always male; however, women often demonstrated noble, heroic behaviors. They supported the heroes and often supplied them with the secrets of life. Ariadne, princess of Crete, told Theseus how to escape from a maze, which saved his life. Medea helped Jason and the Argonauts during their quest and their journey home to Iolcus, a city in Thessaly. One of the few Greek heroines was Atalanta, a brave huntress whose myth is told in Chapter 2.

The aim of the hero's quest was a specific object or action. However, the most important part of the journey was often not the object of the quest itself but that the hero grew and developed during his quest. The quest might not have been for something noble, but the hero always continued to work toward the goal and refused to surrender.

Greek mythology is important for many reasons. These myths help us understand not only Greek history, but also our own civilization, which has strong roots in Greek culture. Many English words are derived from Greek words. Over the centuries, artists have been moved to create statues and paintings of Greek gods and heroes. Greek mythology has inspired writers to create poems, stories, and plays.

The Greek myths about heroes continue to thrill readers of all ages. These stories are filled with danger and excitement. The heroes display feelings common to all humans but they also show superhuman strength. Heroes rise above the challenges they face to conquer monsters, robbers, and other evil villains. Hero myths are particularly important to history, according to mythologist Peter Stillman:

> Many scholars in fields dealing with myth see the hero story as the central motif of all mythology. Certainly it is the dominant one; the hero myth is universally a powerful shaper of beliefs, rituals, and arts. Yet, despite its countless variations, there is only one hero story. And we have all grown up with it, enjoying it a thousand times over in fairy tales, legends, and folk ballads; and in modern poems, stories, novels, movies, and plays.[9]

1

Perseus and the Gorgon Medusa

INTRODUCTION

The goal of the hero Perseus was to kill the Gorgon Medusa. The Gorgons were three sisters, daughters of the sea god Phorcys, and his wife, Ceto, a sea goddess. Two of the sisters, Euryale and Stheno, were immortal, but the third, Medusa, could be killed. These creatures were covered in golden scales and flew on golden wings. Their hair was a mass of writhing snakes. They lived on the farthest side of the mythical western ocean, and they were feared because with only one glance, they could turn people into stone. All around their island home were the petrified forms of animals and people who had had the misfortune of looking at the Gorgons.

Medusa had once been beautiful, with long, golden hair. She was so lovely that she had attracted the sea god Poseidon, who seduced her in one of the temples of Athena, goddess of wisdom and war. Athena was so furious about this disrespectful action that she transformed Medusa into an ugly creature with bulging eyes, a tongue that lolled out of her mouth, and hissing snakes for hair. Medusa was often depicted in this manner on the artwork of ancient Greece.

The myth of Perseus features some cities located in the Argive plain in the eastern Peloponnesus: Mycenae, Tiryns, and Argos. According to the myth, Perseus founded Mycenae, which today is the location of the most impressive Mycenaean-age ruins in Greece. Perseus became king of Tiryns, located five miles south of Mycenae. The story begins in Argos, situated between Mycenae and Tiryns on the Inachus River. Another important location in the myth is the island of Seriphos, also called Seriphus, an actual island in southeastern Greece in the Aegean Sea southeast of Athens.

Perseus obtained information and objects from several divine creatures in this story. The *Graeae*, or Gray Women, were three ancient women who lived at the western edge of the world where the sun never shone. Perseus tricked them into revealing the location of the Nymphs of the North, who possessed the articles that he needed to overcome the Gorgon Medusa. Various types of nymphs appeared throughout Greek mythology. They were divine spirits who lived in a variety of habitats such as rivers, trees, and springs, or wells. The nymphs in this myth lived in the far northern part of the world, in a joyful land filled with happy people who were always celebrating.

A prediction of the oracle at Delphi begins the myth and has important consequences throughout. King Acrisius of Argos, the grandfather of Perseus, bases his actions and decisions on the oracle's prophecy. These decisions have a direct outcome on the birth and life of Perseus and his mother, Danaë.

The characters appearing in this myth are King Acrisius of Argos, his daughter, Danaë, and her son, Perseus. Others are the oracle at Delphi; Zeus, king of the gods; Polydectes, king of Seriphos, and his brother, Dictys; Athena, goddess of wisdom and war; Hermes, the messenger god; the Graeae, or Gray Women; the Nymphs of the North; the Gorgon Medusa and her two sisters; Andromeda, a beautiful princess; and a sea monster.

Perseus and the Gorgon Medusa

King Acrisius of Argos had only one child, a beautiful daughter named Danaë. The king desperately wanted a son, so he went to visit the oracle at Delphi to see what he should do. Unfortunately, the oracle gave him bad news: Acrisius would never father a son. Even worse, predicted the oracle, his own beautiful daughter would give birth to a son who would someday kill him.

Acrisius wanted to try to keep the prophecy from coming true, but the only way he could be sure of accomplishing this goal would be to kill Danaë. He did not dare kill her himself, for the gods would certainly punish him for intentionally killing his own daughter. Instead, Acrisius tried shutting Danae up in an underground chamber. Day after day, she sat in the dark chamber with nothing to do. One night, as Danaë prepared for bed, a most mysterious circumstance occurred. A shower of gold fell from the sky, pouring through the roof of her chamber and landing in her lap. Zeus, the king of the gods, had changed himself into this golden rain, so that he could quietly and secretly enter her chamber. In due time, Danaë gave birth to Zeus' son, whom she called Perseus.

For four years, Danaë, who remained confined to the bronze vault, managed to keep the baby's presence a secret from her father. But one day, Acrisius heard Perseus playing.

"A child," the king cried out. "Who is the father of this child? How could this have happened?"

Danaë smiled proudly at Acrisius. "My Perseus is the son of the mighty Zeus!"

"You are lying!" shouted Acrisius, yet doubt filled his mind. Who else but a god could have entered the vault in which he had kept his daughter locked away? The king was still afraid of angering the gods by killing the young mother and her child. Yet, now that he saw that the oracle had been correct about his daughter bearing a son, Acrisius was even more afraid than ever that the oracle's prophecy would come true unless he tried to prevent it. So Acrisius ordered a wooden box to be built. He locked Danaë and Perseus inside it and set it afloat in the sea.

Fear filled Danaë as she and her child floated alone on the sea, but she held her young son in her arms, comforting him with her embrace. Before long, Perseus slept, wrapped securely in his warm blanket. Through the night, Danaë listened with terror to the waves bumping against the sides of the wooden box. When dawn came, she could not see the brightening skies, trapped as she was inside the windowless chest.

The chest floated toward the island of Seriphos, where Polydectes was king. The king's brother, a kind and gentle fisherman named Dictys, caught the chest in his net. He wondered what kind of treasure might be inside the box. Dictys opened the lid and was stunned to find human treasures inside, Danaë and Perseus. He took them home with him to live, and as Perseus grew up, Dictys taught him how to be a fisherman.

Now the island of Seriphos was rocky, little more than a cliff rising up out of the ocean. Even though it was a small place, it was many years before Polydectes knew of the mother and son who had been brought to live with his brother. But one day, when the king was out hunting, he stopped at the hut of Dictys. Not surprisingly, Polydectes fell in love with the beautiful Danaë, even though by this time, Perseus had reached manhood and she was much older. But Polydectes was a cruel and evil king, and when he asked Danaë to marry him, she refused. Polydectes thought he could force Danaë to marry him if Perseus were not around to protect his mother, so Polydectes concocted a plan to get rid of Perseus. The king pretended he was going to marry someone else. He gathered together all the young men of Seriphos and announced to them, "I am about to marry. Each of you must bring me a fine horse as a wedding gift."

Because Perseus was poor, he did not have a horse. To make up for this lack, he rashly boasted, "O King, I could just as easily bring you the head of the Gorgon Medusa as I could a horse." Medusa was one of three monstrous sisters, the Gorgons, who had snakes instead of hair. These sisters could fly on golden wings. They had wide, staring eyes, so that anyone who looked at the Gorgons turned to stone. Of the three sisters, only Medusa was mortal, but even if Perseus, by the remotest chance, succeeded in killing her, he could never escape her swift-winged sisters.

King Polydectes smiled at the boast of Perseus. "I accept your pledge." He was sure that Perseus would be turned to stone trying to accomplish this impossible task. Then Polydectes would be able to force Danaë to marry him.

Athena, the goddess of wisdom and war, and Hermes, the messenger god, overheard this conversation, and flew down from Mount Olympus, home of the gods, to help Perseus. Athena still hated Medusa for dishonoring her temple.

Hermes gave Perseus a special scimitar, or small, sharp, curved sword. It was so sturdy that it could not be bent or broken. He also told Perseus important information: "The Nymphs of the North are the only ones who can give you the objects you need to defeat Medusa."

"How do I find these nymphs?" Perseus asked.

"The only people who know how to find them are the Graeae, or Gray Women," Hermes said. "They live in a dark land lit neither by sunlight nor moonglow."

"How can I recognize the Graeae?" Perseus wondered.

Hermes answered, "They have only one eye, which they share amongst them. They take turns, each one removing the eye from her forehead when she has used it for a while."

Perseus shook his head in amazement at hearing about such strange beings.

Hermes continued, "Wait until one of the women has removed the eye. Then she will pass it to one of her sisters. Seize the eye and refuse to return it until the Gray Women have told you how to locate the nymphs."

Athena then gave Perseus her polished bronze shield. She told him to hold it like a mirror and view Medusa only in the shield's reflection—never to look directly at her. If he could avoid looking directly at the Gorgon, he would not be turned to stone.

Hermes guided Perseus to the Gray Women, who lived in a cave near the edge of the world. Perseus hid and watched as the Graeae passed their eye amongst themselves. Then, just as one of the Graeae took the eye out of her forehead and made ready to pass it to one of her sisters, Perseus jumped out and, without hesitating, grabbed the eye, leaving all the sisters blind.

For a moment, none of the Graeae understood what had happened. Then they cried out in confusion. "Someone is here. Who has taken our eye?"

"My name is Perseus, and I come from Seriphos, far, far away."

"We need our eye," said the sisters. "What would you have us do to get it back?"

"I need to know where I can find the Nymphs of the North. Tell me this, and I will gladly give you back your eye," Perseus promised.

The Graeae, who were desperate to get back their eye, told him the directions at once, and, as he had promised, Perseus promptly returned their eye. He had to travel to the far north of the world, where the nymphs welcomed him with feasting and celebrations and gave him the three articles he needed to defeat

Medusa: a pair of winged sandals, a cap which made the wearer invisible, and a pouch, or *kibisis*, that always became exactly the right size to accommodate whatever was carried in it.

Armed with these magical gifts, Perseus flew to the edge of the world near the river Ocean, where the Gorgons lived. Luckily, the monsters were asleep. Perseus looked at Medusa's reflection in Athena's shield, beheaded the monster, and put her head in the magic bag.

Wearing the cap that made him invisible, Perseus escaped from the other two Gorgons and flew toward Seriphos. On the

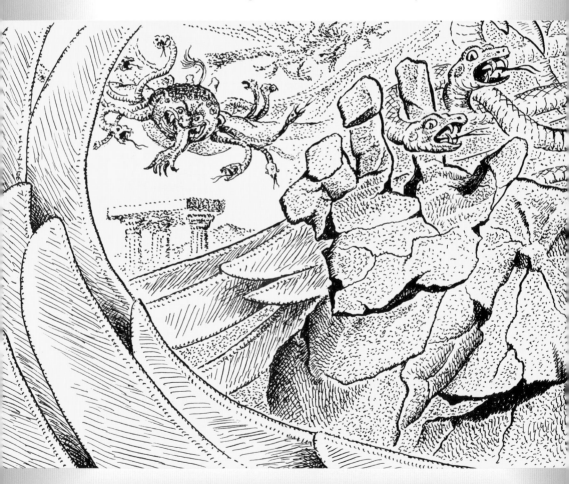

way, he flew over Ethiopia, where he saw Andromeda, a beautiful princess, who was chained to a huge rock. She was in danger of being eaten by a sea monster. No hero could ignore such a challenge. Perseus killed the monster with the scimitar of Hermes and rescued Andromeda, who became his wife.

After the birth of their son Perses, Perseus and Andromeda flew back to Seriphos. There they found Danaë taking refuge at the altar of the gods, for Polydectes was trying to force her to marry him. Dictys had brought Danaë to the altar because it was sacred ground where the king dared not touch her. Perseus

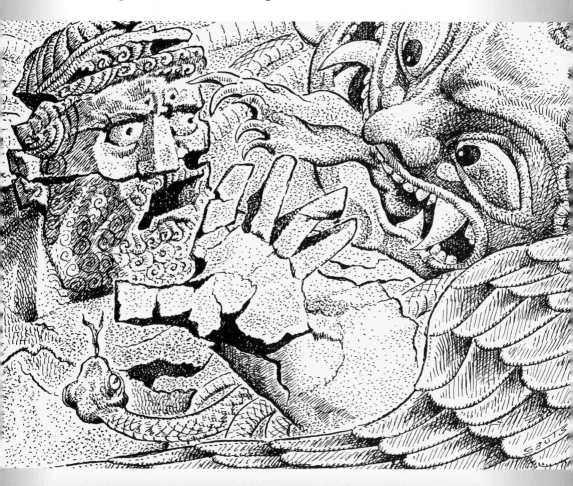

rushed to the king's palace, where he turned Polydectes to stone by showing him Medusa's head. Next, Perseus rewarded Dictys for his loyalty by naming him the new king of Seriphos.

Then, Perseus returned the scimitar to Hermes and gave him the other magical implements to return to the nymphs. To show his thanks to Athena, Perseus mounted Medusa's head on Athena's *aegis*, or breastplate. (This emblazoned shield became the most famous symbol representing Athena.)

Perseus then returned to Argos with his wife and his mother, hoping to make peace with Acrisius, his grandfather. Despite the cruelty Acrisius had shown to Perseus and his mother, Perseus did not desire to exact revenge against his grandfather. However, Acrisius, who had heard all about the mighty deeds of Perseus, was afraid of the young hero. Recalling the oracle's prophecy that he would die at the hand of his grandson, Acrisius fled to Larissa, a city in Thessaly.

Perseus left Andromeda and Danae in Argos and followed Acrisius to Larissa. But before he could find his grandfather, Perseus learned that important athletic games were being held in the city. On impulse, the mighty hero decided to compete in the discus throw, tossing a heavy round disk for distance. When Perseus took his turn throwing, the discus flew into the crowd. It hit Acrisius and killed him. Thus, the oracle's prophecy came to pass.

In sadness, Perseus buried his grandfather with full honors. Even though he had not meant to kill Acrisius, Perseus was too ashamed to return to Argos. Instead, he went to Tiryns, where he became king. He also founded the mighty city of Mycenae and built tall, strong walls around it. Perseus and Andromeda gave birth to another son, Electryon, who later became the grandfather of Heracles, the great Greek hero. They went on to live a life of great happiness, and unlike most other heroes and gods, they remained faithful to each other forever.

QUESTIONS AND ANSWERS

Q: *What did the oracle at Delphi tell King Acrisius of Argos when he asked whether he would ever have a son?*

A: The oracle answered that Acrisius would never have a son. Even worse, his own daughter, Danaë, would give birth to a son who would someday kill Acrisius.

Q: *What did Acrisius do to try to prevent the oracle's warning from coming true?*

A: He locked Danaë in an underground chamber. However, Zeus, the king of the gods, visited her in the form of golden rain, and as a result, she had a son, Perseus, after his visit. When Acrisius found out about Perseus, he locked Danaë and her son in a wooden chest and set it afloat on the sea.

Q: *What happened to Danaë and Perseus after Acrisius tried to dispose of them?*

A: Their chest floated to the island of Seriphos, where they were rescued by the kind fisherman, Dictys, the brother of King Polydectes of Seriphos. They lived with Dictys, who raised Perseus as a fisherman.

Q: *Who was the Gorgon Medusa?*

A: She was a monster with bulging eyes and writhing snakes instead of hair. Anyone or anything that looked at her turned to stone.

Q: *What plan did Polydectes develop to try to force Danaë into marrying him?*

A: He tricked Perseus into promising to bring him the head of the Gorgon Medusa. The king was sure that Perseus would be turned to stone trying to complete this impossible task. Polydectes would then be able to force Danaë to marry him.

Q: *Which Olympian gods helped Perseus and by what means did they help him?*

A: Hermes, the messenger god, lent Perseus a special scimitar and told him that the Nymphs of the North would give him the special objects he needed to conquer the Gorgons. Hermes guided Perseus to the Graeae, or Gray Women, who were the only ones who knew the location of the nymphs. Athena gave Perseus her polished bronze shield and told him to hold it like a mirror and view Medusa only on the shield's reflection to avoid being turned to stone.

Q: *How did Perseus use the advice of the gods and all the magical objects to accomplish his goal of beheading Medusa?*

A: He flew with the winged sandals to the edge of the world, where the Gorgons lived. Looking at Medusa's reflection in Athena's shield, he beheaded the monster with Hermes' scimitar, and put her head in the magic pouch. Wearing the cap that made him invisible and the winged sandals, Perseus escaped from the other two Gorgons.

Q: *After killing Medusa, Perseus completed an exciting rescue. Who did he rescue, how did he do it, and what was the result?*

A: He saw Andromeda, a beautiful princess, who was chained to a huge rock and in danger of being eaten by a sea monster. He killed the monster with the scimitar of Hermes and married the princess.

Q: *What was unusual about the marriage of Perseus and Andromeda?*

A: Unlike most other gods and heroes, they remained faithful to each other.

| *Heroes in Greek Mythology Rock!*

EXPERT COMMENTARY

The myth of Perseus includes perhaps more elements of folklore than any other Greek myth. Edith Hamilton, who wrote numerous books on Greek mythology, noted, "This is a story on the level of the fairy story. Hermes and Athena act like the fairy godmother in *Cinderella*. The magical wallet and cap belong to the properties fairy tales abound in everywhere."[1]

Classicist Barry B. Powell added that the Perseus myth follows typical folktale patterns:

> Of all the Greek legendary cycles, that of Danaë and Perseus is closest to folktale. The early part of the story follows a folktale pattern sometimes called the girl's tragedy, which contains these elements: prohibition, seclusion, violation of the prohibition, threat of punishment or death, and finally liberation. Because of an oracle, Danaë is forbidden to marry (*prohibition*). She is locked in a tower to keep her from men (*seclusion*), but nonetheless becomes pregnant (*violation*). A wicked relative, her father Acrisius, places her and the child in the box (*threat of death*), but she is saved by Dictys (*liberation*).
>
> Perseus' own story follows closely the folktale pattern of the quest, which usually contains these elements: A member of a family is threatened, the hero is sent on a quest, he acquires the use of a magical agent, he reaches his goal in a faraway land, he combats a villain, he is temporarily overcome, he vanquishes the enemy, he is pursued but escapes, he arrives home and is recognized, the villain is punished, and the hero is married and ascends the throne. In the case of Perseus, Polydectes wants to marry Danaë (*threat*), which leads to Perseus' boast that he will bring back the Gorgon's head (*quest*). The hat, sandals, wallet, and scimitar make his task possible (*magical agent*). He reaches the river Ocean (*faraway land*) and beheads Medusa (*combat and victory*); conspicuously missing from this story is the hero's temporary defeat. The immortal Gorgons

come after Perseus (*pursuit*), but he escapes. On Seriphos (*arrival home*) he proves his greatness by holding up the Gorgon's head (*recognition*) and petrifying Polydectes . . . (*villain punished*). He frees Andromeda and takes the kingship of Tiryns (*marriage and ascent to the throne*).[2]

The heroic characteristics of Perseus included not only bravery, but a characteristic that many Greek heroes did not display: virtue. Dana Burgess, a professor of foreign language, classics, and literature, and his coauthor, Kevin Osborn, considered Perseus to be one of the most virtuous heroes in Greek literature:

> A model of chivalry, he rescued his future bride, Andromeda, from a monster and his mother from a lecherous and powerful king. A brave and resourceful adventurer, he ranks among the greatest monster-slayers of classical mythology. A paragon of fidelity—one of the rarest virtues seen in Greek and Roman myths—Perseus remained true to Andromeda throughout their marriage. A beloved king, he not only ruled Tiryns for many years, but founded the neighboring city of Mycenae and fortified Midea as well.[3]

2

Atalanta

INTRODUCTION

Although many female goddesses existed in Greek mythology, Atalanta was one of the few female heroines. This is because of the role that women held in the Greek family. By Hellenistic times (fourth—first century B.C.), the typical Greek family consisted of three children: two boys and one girl. One boy would become a warrior to fight in the continual battles waged between the city-states, while the other boy was to carry on the family name.[1] The girl served a political purpose, for Greek marriages were rarely based on love, but instead on economic needs and political tactics. For each daughter they had, a family had to provide a dowry, the money and goods that a woman brought to her husband in marriage. Because girls did not carry on the family name, it was considered a disadvantage to have more than one girl child. Additional children born to a family might be left in the wild to die because families could not afford to raise them. At the start of this myth, the heroine, Atalanta, has been left on a mountainside to die because her father wanted a baby boy.

Our primary source about the role of women in society is Greek literature; however, this picture is tainted because most literature was composed by males, particularly writers from Athens.[2] (A famous exception is the female poet Sappho from the island of Lesbos; however, only a few fragments of her work remain.) In mythology, the ideal Greek woman was beautiful, submissive, and loyal to her husband. However, according to Greek literature, a woman's true nature was the exact opposite: She would lie, scheme, and cheat to gain power over any male.[3] Marriage, however, was thought to tame a woman's wild nature. Under the guidance of her husband, who had authority over her, a woman would assume the many responsibilities of marriage, including child rearing and management of the household. In so doing, a woman would become submissive and modest—the picture of "perfect womanhood."

In today's world, the standards of behavior applied to women of ancient Greece may seem unfair. Modern women, however, have more control over their economic freedom and have choices about whether to marry or have children. Although the role of Greek women seems restricted, it must be viewed in the context of their times. They did have a relatively high amount of power compared to women of other ancient cultures. In ancient Egypt and Mesopotamia, for example, men took several wives, who competed with each other for power in the household. The Greeks observed monogamy, the practice of marrying only one spouse, and a Greek woman held a position of respect by virtue of being in charge of her household.

In this myth, Atalanta, the noted huntress, had no desire to marry, even though many men wanted to marry her, for she was extremely beautiful. Instead, Atalanta preferred to hunt and compete in athletic contests against men. This description makes her sound like a modern feminist, an individual who believes in the economic, political, and social equality of women. However, we must be careful not to attribute a modern theory to an ancient myth.

Because various versions of this myth have been handed down over the centuries, confusion exists over the names of some of the characters. Some versions tell that Atalanta's father was Schoeneus of Boeotia, a region in Greece north of Attica, the area where Athens is located. Other tales tell that Atalanta's father was Iasus of Arcadia, a region in the Peloponnesus. Atalanta is pursued by a suitor named Melanion (also spelled Milanion), but in some versions of the tale, this suitor is called Hippomenes instead. Because this is a myth rather than history, the exact names are not as important as the roles the characters play in the myth. In the version retold here, Atalanta's father is known as Iasus and her suitor as Melanion. Also featured in this myth are centaurs; Aphrodite, goddess of love and beauty; various suitors; and Zeus, king of the gods.

Atalanta

When Atalanta was born, her father, Iasus of Arcadia, was terribly disappointed, because he had wanted a son to carry on the family name. He left the tiny baby girl exposed on a mountainside, hoping that she would die. Unknown to Atalanta's father, a mother bear found the baby. She kept her warm and nursed her as if she were her own bear cub. Then some hunters found Atalanta and took her to live with them. They taught her how to live as a human being, and she grew into a brave and courageous little girl. The hunters taught her all manner of skills in hunting so that she became adept with a bow and arrow. Her speed in running was rivaled only by her beauty.

One day, when Atalanta went hunting, two centaurs followed her through the woods. Because they were half horse, the centaurs could run much faster than Atalanta, so there was no way she could escape them. She turned and aimed at the centaurs with arrows shot from her bow. The arrows pierced deep into the centaurs' bodies, and they dropped to the ground dead.

When Atalanta was grown, she returned to her father's palace. He wanted her to marry, but she was determined never to take a husband, for she loved to hunt and shoot. She knew that once she married, she would not be able to partake of these pastimes, for she would have to run her household. Still, her father continued to pressure her about taking a husband. Finally, Atalanta agreed to marry whoever could beat her in a foot race, knowing full well that no such man existed.

She chose as a site for the races a large enclosed oval athletic field, or stadium. One at a time, she raced her suitors, giving each of them a head start. Although her suitors had to race unarmed, Atalanta always carried her bow and arrows. When she passed her suitor at the finish line, which she always did, Atalanta immediately shot him with one of her arrows. Then the beautiful maiden chopped off the head of the deceased suitor and placed it on a pole, or staff, which she displayed at the stadium. Soon, the decaying heads of a large number of suitors encircled the stadium. Despite such a daunting display, suitors continued to come and try for Atalanta's hand in marriage.

One day, a young man named Melanion came to watch the suitors racing Atalanta. He had been wondering why any man would risk his life just to obtain a wife, but then he gazed upon Atalanta's splendid face and figure. He fell instantly in love with her and decided, then and there, to try for her hand.

Atlanta had also noticed Melanion, who had a most pleasing appearance. For the first time, she felt doubts about racing one of her suitors. "What is it I feel for him?" she asked herself. "Do I feel pity, or is this love? I have never before pitied any of my suitors for the defeat I was about to inflict upon them. Why do I think of Melanion when no other suitor remains in my mind?"

Melanion prayed to Aphrodite, goddess of love and beauty, to favor his attempt to win the hand of Atalanta. High up on Mount Olympus, home of the gods, Aphrodite heard his prayer. She wanted every woman to marry, so she descended to her sacred island of Cyprus in the eastern Mediterranean. There stood a tree with leaves and apples that shimmered with gold. Aphrodite plucked three apples from the tree and brought them to Melanion, making herself invisible so that only he could see her. "Here, Melanion," Aphrodite said, "take these golden apples. See how they shine? No one can gaze at these pure gold fruits and not want them."

"Thank you, kind Aphrodite," answered Melanion. "Surely with your help, I shall win the race and the hand of Atalanta in marriage."

A crowd gathered at the stadium, and Atalanta and Melanion waited for the signal to start the race. She stood tall, proud, and very beautiful. Melanion tightly gripped his three apples. Then the race was on, and, as was customary, Atalanta gave her suitor a head start. The crowd cheered as Atalanta's and Melanion's feet flew over the earthen track. Then Atalanta sped up and began to pass Melanion, her hair streaming out behind her. Melanion threw one of the golden apples in front of her. The sparkle of the apple caught Atalanta's eye, and she bent down to pick up the unusual fruit. It rolled past her, and she had to briefly step off the running track to pick up the apple. In that moment, Melanion surged past her.

But his lead was temporary. As Atalanta began to pass him a second time, Melanion rolled the second apple into Atalanta's path and again, she bent down to grab it. Once more, Melanion rushed past Atalanta.

Now the finish line was fast appearing. Atalanta caught up with Melanion. Just then, he tossed the third apple with all his might, so that it rolled off the running path. Atalanta had to swerve sideways to reach the golden prize. And in that moment, Melanion crossed the finish line and claimed Atalanta as his bride.

Atalanta realized that she loved Melanion as much as he loved her. In their desire to show their affection for one another, they made love in a nearby shrine of Zeus. This, of course, was forbidden by the gods. In punishment for this act, Zeus turned Atalanta and Melanion into lions, and they could no longer make love to each other, for according to the ancient Greeks, lions could mate with leopards, but not with other lions.

QUESTIONS AND ANSWERS

Q: *Why was Atalanta's father, Iasus, disappointed when she was born?*

A: He wanted a son to carry on the family name, not a daughter.

Q: *What happened after Iasus tried to dispose of Atalanta?*

A: A mother bear found her and nursed her as if she were her own bear cub. Then hunters took Atalanta to live with them and raised her to be a skilled hunter.

Q: *When Atalanta was grown, what did Iasus pressure her to do? What was her response and why?*

A: Iasus wanted Atalanta to marry. She refused, because she wanted to remain a huntress rather than lose her freedom by becoming a wife who had to manage a household.

Q: *How did Atalanta agree to choose a husband?*

A: She agreed to marry whoever could beat her in a foot race, knowing that no such man existed.

Q: *By what means did Atalanta defeat her suitors and what did she do with them afterward?*

A: She gave each suitor a head start and then shot him with her arrows when she won the race. Then, she cut off the deceased suitor's head and displayed it on a pole at the race stadium. Atalanta beat each suitor even though she gave him a head start in the race.

Q: *What happened when Melanion saw Atalanta for the first time?*

A: He fell deeply in love with her and decided he wanted to race against her to try to win her hand in marriage.

Q: *Who helped Melanion and what objects did she use?*

A: The goddess of love and beauty, Aphrodite, brought Melanion three golden apples that she had picked off a golden tree on her island of Cyprus.

Q: *What strategy did Melanion employ in the race against Atalanta?*

A: After the start of the race, just as Atalanta surged ahead of him, Melanion threw down one of the golden apples. Atalanta was attracted by its golden brilliance and bent down to pick it up, which slowed down her progress in the race. Melanion did this again with the second apple. Just before the finish line, he threw the third apple so far that Atalanta had to swerve out of the running path to reach it, and at that moment, Melanion crossed the finish line ahead of Atalanta.

Q: *After Atalanta and Melanion married, what did they do and what were the consequences of this act?*

A: In their desire to show their deep affection for one another, they made love in a nearby shrine of Zeus. This action was forbidden by the gods, so Zeus punished Atalanta and Melanion by turning them into lions.

EXPERT COMMENTARY

In many myths and folktales, a hero or prince sought the hand of a princess in marriage and failed in the attempt. The plot of this myth carries a unique twist, according to Michael Grant, historian and classical scholar, since it "is a curious variant in which the princess herself runs and loses" the race.[4]

Grant also noted:

> There are two stories of Atalanta. The other . . . tells how, after failures by Jason, Pirithous and others, she was the first to wound the monstrous boar of Calydon in Aetolia. The beast was then dispatched by Meleager who gave her the head and hide as a trophy. Ovid treats the heroines of the two tales as the same person, though whether this identification was his own, or inherited by him, cannot be determined.[5]

Edith Hamilton, world-renowned expert in Greek mythology, considered the confusion irrelevant:

> If there were two Atalantas it is certainly remarkable that both wanted to sail on the *Argo*, both took part in the Calydonian boar hunt, both married a man who beat them in a foot race, and both were ultimately changed into lionesses. Since the story of each is practically the same as that of the other it is simpler to take it for granted that there was only one.[6]

Professor Martin P. Nilsson, who studied Greek folk religion, wrote about the role of women in Greek society:

> Greek society was an extremely male society, especially in Athens and the Ionian cities. Women were confined to their houses and seldom went outdoors. But religion did not exclude them. There were priestesses in many cults, and women regularly took part in the festivals and sacrifices . . . Nevertheless, women had only a subordinate position.[7]

3

The Calydonian
Boar Hunt

INTRODUCTION

Every area in Greece had its local heroes and heroines. The legend of the Calydonian Boar Hunt is associated with Aetolia, a region in central Greece north of the entrance to the Gulf of Corinth. Calydon was the capital of Aetolia. Because King Oeneus of Calydon had offended Artemis, goddess of the hunt, childbirth, and the moon, by failing to offer her sacrifices, Artemis sent a wild boar, or sow, to destroy Calydon. Oeneus summoned heroes from all parts of Greece to come and hunt the monster. The beautiful and famous huntress Atalanta also joined the group, even though many of the male hunters did not want her to take part. However, Meleager, the king's son, was attracted to her great beauty and wanted her to participate.

Many local myths, including this one, became famous throughout all of Greece. Meleager's fame as a hero came mainly from his participation in this boar hunt. During Mycenaean times (1600—1200 B.C.), boar hunts were a common and popular activity for the nobility.[1] The myth of the Calydonian Boar Hunt may have gained widespread notice in Greek society because it caused a family member to kill others in the family, which the gods could not let go unpunished.

In Greek mythology, myths about hunting featured a variety of themes, including the similarities between hunting and sacrifice and between hunting and war, and the dangers that hunters faced as well as the dangers that they sometimes presented to society.[2] In the ancient Greek culture, meat was obtained through both hunting and sacrifice. However, the purpose of sacrifice was to ensure positive relationships with the gods, while the goal of the hunt was to obtain food for a meal or to destroy an aggressive animal. In this myth, the hunters seek to kill the Calydonian Boar, a gigantic sow that had been ravaging the countryside around Calydon. Hunting in ancient times resembled war and presented parallel dangers, because in the case of both war and the hunt, a human group was organized to kill an enemy. Although a hunt was organized for the benefit of a community or living group, a hunter sometimes became consumed by the passions of the chase and endangered his fellow hunters or the very community he sought to protect. In this myth, Meleager, the king's son, ignores the traditions of his hunting group by giving the skin of the dead boar to Atalanta because he is attracted to her. As a result of his gift, the goal of the hunting group changes to a warlike one, causing Meleager's own death and that of some of his relatives. Atalanta, as a female, does not belong, and her presence there results in family enmity and ultimate disaster.

Fate, the concept that a person's destiny has already been decided, plays an important role in this myth, as it often did in Greek mythology. In this myth, the Fates, or Moirai, appear. These three daughters of Zeus were portrayed as a trio of old women who were responsible for the destiny of every human. Clotho, or Spinner, spun out the thread of life, which held the fate of each mortal from the moment of birth. Lachesis, or Apportioner, measured out the thread. Atropos, or Inflexible, the smallest and most feared of the Fates, cut it off with her shears and brought life to its conclusion. Because of the involvement of the Fates, many figures in Greek myth were aware of their destiny, yet they acted almost as if it did not matter. In this myth, Meleager's mother at first tried to prevent his fated death. Then she fulfilled the prophecy of the Fates by her actions. Meleager was a hero whose end was destined to be tragic, despite his bravery, physical strength, or skill in hunting.

Characters included in this myth are Oeneus, king of Calydon; Meleager, the king's son; Althaea, Meleager's mother; the Fates; Artemis, goddess of the hunt, childbirth, and the moon; the Calydonian Boar; a large group of hunters; and Atalanta, the huntress.

The Calydonian Boar Hunt

Oeneus was king of Calydon. After his wife, Althaea, bore him a son, whom she named Meleager, the Fates appeared in her bedroom.

The first of the Fates, Clotho, or Spinner, chanted, "Your son is destined to be a famous young man."

The second of the Fates, Lachesis, or Apportioner, added, "Meleager will be known for his great courage."

The last of the Fates, Atropos, or Inflexible, walked over to the hearth where logs lay burning. She spoke in an eerie voice as she pointed to one of the logs. "Let this be a warning," she said. "Do you see this blazing log?"

After Althaea nodded in agreement, Atropos continued. "When flames totally consume that log, your son, Meleager, will perish."

"No, please do not put such a curse on my son," Althaea begged. But the Fates had already disappeared.

Althaea grabbed the log and put out the flames. She flung the log into the bottom of a chest that she hid in a closet deep within the palace. She thought that by hiding the log she could prevent the curse from happening.

As Meleager grew to manhood, he was raised to be a king. He developed heroic qualities, growing to be strong and handsome. He became an excellent hunter, for he practiced long hours throwing his spear and shooting arrows with his bow, and his bravery was unquestioned.

Meleager's father, King Oeneus, whose name meant "wineman," was the first man in Greece to grow grapes. Every year, he offered a sacrifice of the first grapes of that year's harvest to the gods. But one year, Oeneus forgot to include Artemis, goddess of the hunt, childbirth, and the moon, when he made his sacrifices. Artemis was furious that Oeneus had forgotten to place a sacrifice on her altar. In revenge, she sent the Calydonian Boar, a gigantic wild hog, to destroy Calydon. The boar had fiery eyes, a foaming mouth, and sharp, white tusks. She terrorized the countryside, trampling cornfields and ripping grapes from their fruit-laden vines. She had already slaughtered several men who had tried to kill her.

Oeneus bid the bravest young men of Greece to hunt the boar. Meleager, the son of Oeneus, was part of this group of mighty heroes. When Atalanta, the famous athlete and huntress, arrived to join the hunt, Meleager was attracted to her, for she was lovelier than any other woman he had ever seen. Her hair was bound in a knot at the back of her neck, and her clothing, although simple, fit her to perfection. Atalanta carried a powerful, well-strung bow along with an ivory quiver, or arrow holder, full of arrows. Meleager exercised his role as a leader and the son of a king and insisted that Atalanta be included in the group of hunters, even though some of the heroes did not want to hunt with a woman, for they considered it beneath them.

Armed with swords and shields, lances and double-headed axes, the hunters set out through the forest to find the boar. They did not rush in to attack her in her lair, for they were experienced fighters. Instead, they crashed their spears against their shields, hoping that the noise would drive the boar out into the open so that they could attack her. This technique worked only too well, for the hunters did not know the size and speed of the mighty Calydonian Boar. She came charging out of her wooded hiding place, right into the middle of the hunters. With her slashing tusks, the boar gored several warriors to death. Others she slashed with her sharp hooves. But Atalanta got in close and fired an arrow into the boar's terrible eye. Any other beast would have dropped dead from the wound, but the Calydonian Boar struggled to her feet,

ready to charge again. Just then, Meleager came at the monster with his sword, plunging it deep into the boar's back and repeatedly piercing the boar's body with his spear until she finally died.

Meleager knelt beside the carcass of the great boar and skinned her hide. Now, this hide was a great trophy of the hunt, and Meleager, instead of keeping it for himself as a reward for killing the beast, chose to give it to Atalanta. He did this in part because she had drawn first blood in the victory over the boar, so the hide honored her skill and bravery during the hunt. But Meleager was also so in love with Atalanta that he hoped that his gift would cause her to look upon him with favor. Unfortunately, Meleager's generosity angered many of the hunters, including his mother's brothers, Toxeus and Plexippus, who protested loudly that a woman should not receive such a trophy. If Meleager did not want the hide, they felt that they, by rights of their birth, deserved the trophy. Meleager was furious with the words of his uncles. He quickly drew his sword and plunged it into the heart of Toxeus. Before Plexippus had a chance to ponder whether or not he should fight back, Meleager had stabbed him to death as well.

At the palace, Althaea learned of the success of the hunt. She brought gifts to the gods for her son's safe return. But then she was stunned to see the bodies of her dead brothers brought into the city. When she learned that Meleager was responsible for their deaths, Althaea flew into a rage. "How could you kill my dear brothers?" she screamed at Meleager, even though he was her son.

Consumed with thoughts of revenge, Althaea ran to the hidden trunk and took out the log she had concealed long ago. She threw it onto the fire that she had burning that day. As the log was consumed in flames, Meleager felt scorching pain fill his body. But as befitted a hero, Meleager bore his pain with dignity. He only regretted that he could not have died in battle. As the log expired in the flames, so, too, did Meleager, just as the Fates had prophesied.

QUESTIONS AND ANSWERS

Q: *What did Oeneus do to defeat the Calydonian Boar?*

A: Oeneus called on Greece's finest young heroes to join his son, Meleager, to hunt down the boar.

Q: *Why did the hunters resent Atalanta?*

A: Many of these male heroes did not want to hunt with a woman because they considered it beneath them.

Q: *After Meleager skinned the boar's hide, what did he do with it and why?*

A: He presented it to Atalanta for drawing first blood in the hunt and to honor her bravery. Meleager hoped to gain Atalanta's favor by giving her this prize of honor.

Q: *How did the other hunters react when Meleager gave the boar's hide to Atalanta?*

A: Many of them were angry. They felt that a woman should never receive the trophy of a hunt. If Meleager did not want the hide, Toxeus and Plexippus felt that they, as family members who had participated in the hunt, were entitled to it.

Q: *How did Meleager react to the angry response of Toxeus and Plexippus?*

A: He killed both of them.

Q: *When Althaea learned of her brothers' deaths, what did she do and what was the result?*

A: Althaea ran to the hidden trunk and removed the log she had stored there just after Meleager's birth. She threw it on the fire burning that day, and as the Fates had predicted, Meleager died when the log burned out.

EXPERT COMMENTARY

The role of fate in Greek mythology is fascinating to analyze, according to classics professors Mark P. O. Morford and Robert J. Lenardon:

> Fate is often thought of in the singular (Greek, *Moira*), in a conception that is much more abstract and more closely linked to a profound realization of the roles played by Luck or Fortune (*Tyche*) and Necessity (*Ananke*) in the scheme of human life. The relation of the gods to destiny is variously depicted and intriguing to analyze in the literature. According to some authors Zeus is supreme and controls all, but others portray a universe in which even the great and powerful Zeus must bow to the inevitability of Fate's decrees. The depth of this feeling of the Greeks for the working of Moira or the Moirai cannot be overemphasized. It provides a definite and unique tone and color to the bulk of their writing. One thinks immediately of Homer or Herodotus or the tragedians, but no major author was untouched by fascination with interrelation of god, mortals, and fate and the tantalizing interplay of destiny and free will.[3]

Morford and Lenardon add, "The Romans developed this same tragic view of human existence. For them Fate is personified by the Parcae, or more abstractly conceived as Fatum (Fate)."[4]

Authors Donna Rosenberg and Sorelle Baker compared the intertwining of an individual's fate with an inanimate object in this myth to similar situations in other cultures:

> In Celtic and Norse cultures, a person's life source also may be connected to an object outside of his body, such as to a plant or an animal. In each situation, whatever happens to the object happens to the person whose life is connected with it.[5]

4

Jason and the Argonauts

INTRODUCTION

The legend of Jason and the Argonauts is probably older than Homer's *Iliad* and *Odyssey*. In the twelfth book, or chapter, of the *Odyssey*, which was composed in the eighth century B.C., the story of the voyage is already a familiar tale. Today, the most widely used literary source, and the one on which this myth is based, is the *Argonautika* of the Greek poet Apollonius of Rhodes (295—215 B.C.).[1]

Jason was a member of the ruling family of Iolcus, a city located at the base of Mount Pelion in Thessaly. Jason's family was descended from Hellen, ancestor of all the Greeks. Jason's grandfather, Cretheus, married Tyro and together they had three sons, including Jason's father, Aeson. Tyro also fell in love with the sea god Poseidon, and they had twin sons, Pelias and Neleus. Pelias was a greedy, power hungry man who took away the throne of Iolcus from Jason's father, the rightful heir, and tried to get rid of Jason by sending him on a near-impossible mission to obtain the Golden Fleece.

The Golden Fleece was the hide of a ram that had been sacrificed to Zeus. The hide glowed with an unearthly red sheen and represented supernatural powers and kingship.[2] The ram's pelt was hung on a sacred oak tree that was located at the opposite end of the known world from Iolcus in a town called Colchis.

Jason sailed on the mighty *Argo*, meaning "swift," a vessel crafted from timber harvested from Mount Pelion. The prow, or front, was carved from part of a sacred oak tree from the sanctuary of Zeus at Dodona, a shrine in a remote area of northern Greece. This piece of oak could speak prophecies. Apollonius described the *Argo* as being equipped with oars lashed to benches on which the heroes sat to row. It also had a sturdy mast and well-made sails. Similar ships were depicted on ancient vases.

The crew of the *Argo* was made up of the mightiest heroes and young nobles of the Greek world. There were about fifty

Argonauts; however, different sources list different names because storytellers modified the tale to make sure that a hero from their city or region was included in the crew. In all versions of the myth, however, the main characters are the same. Jason was always the heroic leader. Argos, the master builder, oversaw the building of the ship. Tiphys was the helmsman who steered the vessel. Other Argonauts were Orpheus, the musician; Zetes and Calaïs, the sons of the North Wind; the twins Castor and Polydeuces; and Heracles, the greatest of Greek heroes.

A centaur, the Harpies, and nymphs were also featured in this myth. A centaur had a human head and chest, and the legs and body of a horse. Usually, centaurs were wild and uncivilized, but Chiron, the centaur in this tale, was gentle and educated. The Harpies, whose name means "the snatchers," were part woman and part bird. These demons snatched food with their sharp talons and crooked beaks and befouled whatever crumbs remained with a disgusting smell. Nymphs, a type of divine spirit, were commonly depicted as beautiful young girls who loved to sing and dance. Often, they were attendants for the major gods or goddesses.

The perpetual interference of the gods in human affairs occurs often in this tale. Typically, the gods had their favorites whom they supported. In this myth, Hera, queen of the gods, does all she can to help Jason. The gods also took offense when mortals forgot, or, even worse, deliberately chose not to honor them. Pelias, the evil king of Iolcus, did not render to Hera what she felt was the honor due her, so throughout the myth, she attempts to destroy Pelias.

The plot is typical of folktales: Jason, the hero, is given a number of nearly impossible tasks to perform; he successfully completes them; he is helped by the local princess, whom he later takes as his bride.[3] He sometimes ponders his ability to complete his task. He receives help from Medea, a witch, and from the gods. This dependence and occasional lack of confidence could be viewed as a flaw, or it could be considered "a realistic acceptance of man's limitations."[4]

Jason and the Argonauts

The tale of Jason and the Golden Fleece began long before Jason was born. Aeolus, the son of Hellen, the ancestor of all the Greeks, had seven sons, including Athamas. Athamas became king of the town of Orchomenus in Boeotia, a plain north of Attica. He took as his first wife Nephele, and she bore him two children, a son, Phrixus, and a daughter, Helle. When Athamas tired of Nephele, he took a new wife, Ino, who bore their two sons. Because Phrixus was next in line to inherit the throne instead of Ino's sons, Ino decided to kill Phrixus.

Ino secretly plotted with local women to parch all of the seed grain, so that after it was sown, no crops grew. Famine filled the land, so Athamas sent messengers to Apollo's oracle at Delphi to ask for advice. Ino intercepted the messengers when they returned from Delphi and bribed them to tell Athamas that Apollo wanted him to sacrifice Phrixus if he ever hoped the famine would cease.

In deep sadness, Athamas led Phrixus to the sacrificial altar. Helle stood close by, consumed with grief. Just as Athamas lifted the knife to stab Phrixus, a ram with a golden hide flew down to the altar. Phrixus and Helle scrambled onto the ram's back, and it soared away to the east. Unfortunately, above the straits, between Europe and Asia, Helle lost her grip, fell into the water, and drowned. (These waters, named after Helle, are still known today as the Hellespont.) The ram flew on, with Phrixus gripping tightly to its hide, until it reached the town of Colchis at the eastern end of the Black Sea. King Aeëtes ruled Colchis, and he and his people were fierce and mighty. Yet they welcomed Phrixus as a guest, in the tradition of Greek hospitality. Phrixus sacrificed the ram to Zeus in thanks for his safe flight and gave the fleece to the king. Aeëtes hung it from an oak tree in a sacred grove, where it was guarded by a serpent that never slept.

Now Cretheus, the brother of Athamas, was king of Iolcus, a seaport in Thessaly. When he died, his son Aeson, as the rightful heir, was expected to ascend the throne. But Pelias, the stepson of Cretheus, was more powerful than Aeson, and he usurped, or stole away, the throne from Aeson. Pelias, who was power hungry and evil, imprisoned Aeson in the castle at Iolcus.

Soon after Pelias took control of the throne, Polymede, the wife of Aeson, gave birth to a son, Jason. Jason was rightfully the next in line to inherit the throne after his father, Aeson. But Pelias was now in control and had sons of his own. Polymede feared that Pelias might kill Jason, to make sure that one of his sons would ultimately succeed him to the throne. To ensure her baby's safety, Polymede spread the tale that he was stillborn. Then she secretly sent Jason away to be raised by a centaur, Chiron, who lived nearby on the slopes of Mount Pelion. Chiron taught Jason heroic skills such as archery and wrestling, and raised him to be strong and brave.

During the time that Jason was growing up, the Delphic oracle gave an ominous warning to Pelias. Pelias learned that he would die at the hands of one of his kinsmen, who would approach him wearing just one sandal.

After twenty years, Jason came down from Mount Pelion, determined to claim the throne that should rightfully have been his. Jason set off for Iolcus, but before Jason reached the city, he came to the River Anarus. The waters of the river were swollen with the rains, and an old woman crouched by the stream, hesitating to cross the dangerous waters. Jason hoisted her across his muscular shoulders and safely carried her across. In the process, though, Jason lost one of his sandals in the stream. He decided that it was useless to look for the sandal, for surely the rushing waters would have carried it away. Jason continued on his journey to Iolcus, never realizing that by helping the old woman, he had made an important decision that would affect his life forever.

The old crone was Hera, queen of the gods, in disguise. She already hated haughty King Pelias because he had never treated her with respect or offered sacrifices in her honor. Hera was waiting by the river because she wanted to find an honorable man to use as her tool in seeking revenge against Pelias. Because of Jason's kindness in helping her, Hera decided he was the perfect candidate. She also decided to protect Jason in whatever way she could.

The people of Iolcus stared as Jason entered their city, for he presented a magnificent picture of strength. A leopard's skin covered his shoulders and shiny locks of hair graced his head. Heedless of his missing sandal, Jason boldly entered the royal palace and stood before King Pelias. "I have come to regain the honor of my family," Jason told Pelias. "You had no right to take the throne that was my father's. I have come to claim it back for my father, and for myself."

Pelias looked upon Jason with fear, because the young hero represented a fulfillment of the oracle's prophecy. Jason was a relative, and he wore only one sandal. Pelias thought quickly. He wanted to keep his throne at all costs. He knew that he had never been a popular king. Realistically, he understood that the people of Iolcus might gladly replace him with the attractive youth who now stood before him, a youth who might very well kill Pelias. The evil king promised to give up the throne if Jason would first fetch the Golden Fleece from King Aeëtes. Pelias felt certain that Jason would never be able to convince King Aeëtes to give up the fleece. Nor did he believe that Jason could even safely complete

the dangerous journey to Colchis, which was located at the other end of the known world. Thus, King Pelias thought he was clever in making a promise he would never have to keep.

Rather than deter him, however, the idea of such a challenging journey sparked Jason's sense of adventure. He was not the only one to crave adventure, however. He sent out a call for the best fighting men of the day to join him in Iolcus. Soon, he had pieced together a heroic crew of about fifty men. Before long, they became known as the Argonauts, named after their mighty ship, the *Argo*. The Argonauts included Heracles, already famed for completing many heroic deeds, and Orpheus, the musician son of the god Apollo.

Jason led his crew aboard the *Argo*, striding on deck as proudly as a god. The swift vessel left with its talking prow, or front, crying out in its eagerness to seek adventure. After leaving Iolcus, the Argonauts rowed north along the coast of Greece and passed Mount Pelion on the west. As a stiff breeze came up, the crew put up the sails and the *Argo* headed due east across the Aegean Sea, through the narrow Hellespont, and into the Propontis, the body of water connecting the Hellespont with the Black Sea. (The Propontis is now called the Sea of Marmara.)

All the Argonauts put their energies into rowing hard, but Heracles was especially eager to show off his mighty strength. He pulled so hard that he snapped his oar in two, and the *Argo* had to stop in Cios, a city on the Asiatic shore of the Propontis, so that Heracles could cut another oar from a fir tree. Hylas, who served Heracles as a squire, or manservant, went to a nearby spring to get some water. The nymphs, or water spirits, who lived in the spring pulled Hylas down into the water, so that they could keep the handsome young man with them forever. When Hylas failed to bring the water, Heracles began a search for his young servant. Finally, the *Argo* sailed without Heracles. (He eventually returned to Iolcus on his own, never having found Hylas.)

The next morning, the Argonauts continued on their journey. The *Argo* sailed for a day and a night and put in at the land of the Bebryces, a fierce warrior tribe. Their king, Amycus, boasted that he had never lost a boxing match to anyone who visited his land. Jason chose Polydeuces, the best boxer of all the Argonauts, to face Amycus. Polydeuces dealt Amycus a mighty blow to the ear, crushing the bones of the boastful king into his brain.

The next day, the *Argo* sailed into the turbulent Bosporus, the narrow channel joining the Propontis with the Black Sea. On the day following, the Argonauts moored their ship at Salmydessus, a city in Thrace, a region northeast of Greece. This land was ruled by King Phineus, a blind prophet. Zeus had blinded Phineus to punish him for revealing too much of the future to the Greeks. Zeus also sent the winged Harpies to forever snatch the food from the hands or mouth of the wretched king. After these monsters grabbed the food with their crooked beaks, they spread a terrible stench over any remaining morsels. Jason formed a plan for the next time that the Harpies flew down to steal away the food of Phineus. Two Argonauts, Zetes and Calaïs, the winged sons of the North Wind, flew after the monsters with drawn swords and forced the Harpies to promise never again to bother Phineus.

Phineus was so grateful that he told Jason how to avoid the dangers of the Symplegades, or Clashing Rocks, two huge boulders located at the northern edge of the Black Sea. Strong winds often caused the rocks to crash together, crushing anything caught between them. Phineus told Jason to release a dove directly between the Clashing Rocks. If the dove flew safely between them, then the *Argo* could sail through safely. As soon as the rocks separated, the crew should row as hard as they could and sail between the rocks.

The next morning, Jason followed the prophet's guidance and released a dove between the Symplegades. When the dove flew between the Clashing Rocks, it lost only a few tail feathers.

Immediately, Jason commanded the ship to follow. As the men rowed hard, waves splashed over their heads, and the boulders loomed so high above them that the sky seemed black. Just when it appeared that the ship might be crushed, it squeezed through the opening at the end of the Symplegades. Only part of an ornament from the stern, or back, of the ship was caught between the rocks. From that day onward, the Clashing Rocks also remained stuck together, for the gods had decreed that they would remain affixed if any ship safely passed between them.

Grateful for their narrow escape, the Argonauts vowed continued support for their leader, Jason. They sailed for several weeks through the Black Sea along the coast of Asia Minor. After several more adventures, they arrived at the eastern end of the Black Sea at the mouth of the river Phasis and sailed up the river to Colchis. They spent the night on board ship, not knowing what they would face the next morning when they met King Aeëtes of Colchis. Jason knew he could rely on his own courage. He also knew that he could rely on his trusty crew, for every Greek hero was committed to follow his leader into battle or any sort of danger they might face.

Unbeknownst to Jason, the Olympian gods were plotting to make sure that he succeeded on his quest. Hera, queen of the gods, knew that he would face hostility from King Aeëtes of Colchis, for he distrusted strangers. She asked Aphrodite, goddess of love, to convince her son Eros, the god of love, to make Aeëtes' daughter, Medea, fall in love with Jason. Medea, who was a sorceress, knew how to work very powerful magic. Hera was sure that if Medea was in love with Jason, she would use her magic to help the Argonauts.

The next morning, Jason explained to King Aeëtes that he and his men were not there to harm King Aeëtes. All they wanted to do was to take the Golden Fleece back to King Pelias. But anger filled the heart of King Aeëtes, because he hated foreigners. An oracle had warned him that a stranger would do him great harm. Aeëtes feared that this stranger, Jason, might be his undoing. The king had no intention of giving up the fleece, so he decided to do whatever he could to prevent Jason from obtaining it. "I will give you the fleece, but only if you can complete these tasks," Aeëtes told Jason. "These tasks are ones that I can do bare-handed. First, you must yoke a pair of fire-breathing bulls and use them to plow a vast field. Then you must sow the field with the teeth of a dragon."

While Jason doubted whether the king could perform these feats, the leader of the Argonauts felt certain that he could accomplish these two challenges, or any others that the king might throw at him. Had he not just sailed all this way with his trusty ship, successfully facing many dangers?

Then Aeëtes set one more task before Jason. "Once you have sowed the dragon's teeth, armed men will spring up from them. You must put to death every one of these warriors."

Jason agreed to take on these tasks, even though he knew he might die trying to accomplish them. However, as a true hero, he was determined to accomplish his quest.

Aeëtes smiled to himself. He was certain that Jason would never be able to complete these challenges. The king had bargained without the knowledge that there were Olympian gods helping Jason. Eros shot an invisible arrow of love into Medea's heart, and she fell deeply in love with the young hero. Without telling her father, Medea gave Jason a magical ointment that would protect him from flames or iron weapons— but only for one day. The next day, Jason spread the ointment on his body and over his weapons.

King Aeëtes and the Argonauts gathered to watch Jason harness the fire-breathing bulls. Along with his spear and shield, Jason carried a glittering helmet and sharp sword. With head held high, he marched down to the cave where the oxen waited. The pair of beasts charged out, breathing flames. The

Argonauts trembled at this sight, but Jason stood his ground, unshaken, keeping his shield before him. The oxen blasted him with their fiery breath, yet the ointment protected Jason. Aeëtes stared in amazement at Jason's mighty strength as the young hero seized the horns of the oxen and forced them into the yoke. The oxen snorted and raged, but Jason prodded them with his spear until the field was plowed with the dragon's teeth. To the cheers of the Argonauts, Jason released the oxen that fled to the lowlands nearby.

By now, armed men had sprouted up in the furrows. They carried sturdy shields and lances. Jason bent and picked up a rock from the ground, a boulder so large that four ordinary men could not have lifted it. He heaved the rock into the middle of the warriors, who turned in confusion to face the source of this sound. With the warriors thus distracted from attacking him, Jason pulled out his sword and slashed them down until not a single warrior was left standing.

Aeëtes stormed back to his palace, furious that Jason had fearlessly accomplished all the tasks set before him. The evil king was now even more determined to destroy Jason in some other way, and vowed to himself that he would never give up the Golden Fleece to the young hero.

That night, Medea stole away from the palace, for she realized that she was in danger of having her father discover how she had helped Jason. By now, Medea was so much in love with Jason that she was more faithful to him than to her father. She warned Jason that, because Aeëtes planned to kill the Argonauts, Jason needed to leave right away to get the Golden Fleece. Jason promised to marry Medea if he successfully completed his quest.

Then Jason, Medea, and the Argonauts all climbed aboard the *Argo* and rowed up the river to the mighty oak upon which the Golden Fleece was hung. Jason and Medea approached the hissing serpent who guarded the fleece. Medea sprinkled drops of a magical potion into the serpent's eyes. Soon the beast was unconscious. Then Jason nimbly climbed up the oak tree and retrieved the Golden Fleece. Jason then told Medea that they needed to make haste to return to the *Argo*. Dawn was breaking when they made it back to the ship. The Argonauts marveled at how the fleece glowed with a bright radiance.

When Aeëtes learned that the fleece was gone, he sent his son, Apsyrtus, and a fleet of warships after Jason and his Argonauts. Medea sent a message to her brother telling him to meet her on a nearby island, because she wanted to go back home with him. She promised to bring the Golden Fleece. Jason hid near the meeting place and ambushed Apsyrtus when he arrived, slashing Medea's brother to pieces with his sword. Jason, Medea, and the Argonauts fled up the Danube River. When the rest of the Colchians learned of the prince's death, they pursued the Argonauts in great fury. However, the goddess Hera again interfered, for she was determined to continue to help Jason. She threw down lightning upon the Colchians, who gave up the chase.

As the *Argo* tried to sail south through the Adriatic Sea, a storm forced the ship north up the mythical Eridanus River, across to the Rhone River, and then back to the Mediterranean Sea. Then Jason and his crew approached the island where the Sirens lived. These winged women sang so sweetly that they had lured many sailors to their deaths. The Sirens' songs were so entrancing that they could stop sailors from performing any actions. As they listened to the music, the sailors forgot all about sailing and eventually starved to death. Luckily, the Argonauts had Orpheus on board. As the *Argo* approached the Sirens, Jason had Orpheus sing and play his lyre, a stringed instrument, which drowned out the music of the Sirens. Right after this, the *Argo* had to sail between Scylla, a six-headed monster who lived in a cave in a cliff, and Charybdis, a deadly whirlpool. Hera, still helping Jason, sent sea nymphs to guide the *Argo* safely through these two dangers.

Heroes in Greek Mythology Rock!

Heading south, a storm drove the Argonauts to the coast of Libya in Africa. A gigantic wave tossed the ship inland, and Jason ordered the Argonauts to lift the ship on their shoulders and carry it over the burning sands. They carried it for nine days until they reached Lake Tritonis. There, the water god Triton guided them back to the Mediterranean, where they finally landed again at Iolcus. Jason's voyage had lasted four months, and many people, including Pelias, had thought that the ship would never return.

Jason brought the Golden Fleece to Pelias. The young hero was stunned to learn that while he was gone, Pelias had forced Aeson, Jason's father, to kill himself. As a result, Jason's mother, Polymede, had run screaming into the palace, cursed Pelias, and stabbed herself to death with a sword.

Pelias accepted the Golden Fleece, but, not surprisingly, refused to honor his promise to return the throne to Jason. Then, Jason and Medea plotted to heap revenge on Pelias. Pelias thought that if he could stay young, he could hold on to his power forever. Jason and Medea convinced him that they had a way to do this. It required the help of the daughters of Pelias. First, Medea cut an old ram into pieces and threw the pieces in a cauldron, which she had secretly filled with magic herbs. When the water boiled, the ram turned into a lamb. Convinced this same process would restore vigorous youth to their father, the daughters of Pelias cut him into pieces and tossed them, just like the ram's, into the boiling cauldron. However, this time Medea failed to add the magic herbs and Pelias remained dead.

So evil King Pelias met his end, as the oracle had prophesied, through the actions of a relative, Jason, who approached him wearing just one sandal. However, despite achieving his quest for the Golden Fleece, Jason never became the king of Iolcus, for the people of that city drove Jason and Medea out for their role in the death of Pelias.

QUESTIONS AND ANSWERS

Q: *What was the Golden Fleece and what did it symbolize?*

A: It was the hide of the golden ram that safely brought Phrixus to Colchis. It represented supernatural powers and kingship.

Q: *Who was Jason?*

A: He was the son of Aeson and Polymede and part of the royal family of Iolcus. He was the rightful heir to the throne after his father.

Q: *While Jason was growing up, the Delphic oracle made a prophecy to Pelias. What was it?*

A: The oracle predicted that Pelias would die at the hands of a relative who approached him wearing just one sandal.

Q: *On the way to Iolcus, Jason met an old woman. Who was she?*

A: She was Hera, queen of the gods, in disguise as an old woman.

Q: *When Jason carried Hera across the River Anarus, what did his effort symbolize?*

A: It demonstrated to Hera that he was an honorable man. She decided that she would protect Jason whenever possible, and use him to seek her revenge against Pelias.

Q: *When Jason confronted Pelias at the palace, why did Pelias fear him?*

A: He knew that Jason, who met Pelias wearing one sandal, was related to him. Thus, Jason represented a possible threat to Pelias as someone who might fulfill the prophecy of the oracle at Delphi.

Q: *What did Pelias demand that Jason do before Pelias would give up the throne to him? What did Pelias hope to accomplish with this demand?*

A: He told Jason that he had to fetch the Golden Fleece from King Aeëtes of Colchis. The journey to Colchis, located at the far end of the known world, would be dangerous. Pelias thought he was being clever in promising to give up his throne, because he believed the task he had assigned would be too difficult for Jason to accomplish.

Q: *How did Jason respond to the challenge to fetch the Golden Fleece?*

A: Reacting with eagerness, Jason assembled a crew of fifty heroes, the Argonauts, and sailed toward Colchis on a swift ship, the *Argo*.

Q: *When Jason arrived in Colchis, what did he ask of King Aeëtes? What did Aeëtes say?*

A: Jason asked for the Golden Fleece. Aeëtes refused to relinquish it unless Jason completed three tasks. He had to yoke a pair of fire-breathing oxen and sow a field with dragon's teeth. Once the field was sown, armed men would spring up. Jason had to kill these warriors.

Q: *How did the gods intervene to help Jason complete the tasks that Aeëtes had given him?*

A: Hera convinced Aphrodite, goddess of love, to ask her son Eros, god of love, to make Medea fall in love with Jason. Eros shot an invisible arrow of love into Medea's heart, and she fell deeply in love with Jason.

Q: *What heroic skills did Jason use to complete his tasks?*

A: He bravely faced the charging oxen without flinching. After seizing the oxen by the horns, he yoked them and plowed the field easily by prodding the oxen with his spear. When armed men sprung up, Jason threw a heavy rock into their midst, a rock so large that four ordinary men could not have lifted it. The confused warriors turned to face the rock, and Jason then slashed them to death with his sword.

Q: *When Jason returned to Iolcus, what bad news did he learn about his parents?*

A: Pelias had forced Aeson, Jason's father, to kill himself. Jason's mother, Polymede, had cursed Pelias and then stabbed herself to death.

Q: *Pelias accepted the Golden Fleece, but refused to give Jason the throne. How did Jason react?*

A: With the help of Medea, Jason plotted revenge against Pelias. Pelias wanted to stay in power and to do so, he needed to stay young. Medea showed the daughters of Pelias how this could be done. She cut an old ram into pieces and boiled the pieces in a cauldron that she had secretly filled with magic herbs. A young lamb bounced out. Then Pelias' daughters cut Pelias into pieces and tossed them into the cauldron. Because Medea did not add magic herbs this time, Pelias died.

Q: *What did the death of Pelias represent?*

A: It fulfilled the prophecy of the oracle, who said that Pelias would die through the actions of a relative who approached him wearing one sandal.

Heroes in Greek Mythology Rock!

EXPERT COMMENTARY

Joseph Campbell, who was a noted expert and writer on mythology, described how a hero, having achieved his quest, must still return with the object or goal of the quest. He wrote that if the goal "has been attained against the opposition of its guardian, or if the hero's wish to return to the world has been resented by the gods . . . then the last stage of the mythological round becomes a lively, often comical, pursuit. This flight may be complicated by marvels of magical obstruction."[5] Campbell called such flight "magic flight" or "obstacle flight," noting:

> One of the most shocking obstacle flights is that of the Greek hero, Jason. He had set forth to win the Golden Fleece. Putting to sea in the magnificent Argo with a great company of warriors, he had sailed in the direction of the Black Sea, and though delayed by many fabulous dangers, arrived, at last, miles beyond the Bosporus, at the city and palace of King Aeetes. Behind the palace was the grove and tree of the dragon-guarded prize.

> Now the daughter of the king, Medea, conceived an overpowering passion for the illustrious foreign visitor and, when her father imposed an impossible task as the price of the Golden Fleece, compounded charms that enabled him to succeed. . . . The infatuated young woman conducted Jason to the oak from which hung the Fleece. . . . Then Jason snatched the prize, Medea ran with him, and the Argo put to sea. But the king was soon in swift pursuit. . . . She persuaded Jason to kill Apsyrtus. . . . Meanwhile the Argo ran with the wind. . . .[6]

Noted Greek mythologist Edith Hamilton described Jason's dangerous voyage and his leadership:

> The first hero in Europe who undertook a great journey was the leader of the Quest of the Golden Fleece. He was supposed to have

lived a generation earlier than the most famous Greek traveler, the hero of the *Odyssey*. It was of course a journey by water. Rivers, lakes, and seas were the only highways; there were no roads. All the same, a voyager had to face perils not only on the deep sea, but on the land as well. Ships did not sail by night, and any place where sailors put in might harbor a monster or a magician who could work more deadly harm than storm and shipwreck. High courage was necessary to travel, especially outside of Greece.

No story proved this fact better than the account of what the heroes suffered who sailed in the ship Argo to find the Golden Fleece. In may be doubted, indeed, if there ever was a voyage on which sailors had to face so many and such varied dangers. However, they were all heroes of renown, some of them the greatest in Greece, and they were quite equal to their adventures.[7]

Writer, translator, and professor Peter Green noted:

Jason and the Argonauts' quest for the Golden Fleece is probably the oldest extant Greek myth. At one level this story is a classic fairy tale: The young prince is sent on a perilous expedition and triumphs over the obstacles put in his path–from clashing rocks to fire-breathing bulls–to win not only the fleece but also the hand of Medea, the daughter of King Aeëtes. . . .[8]

Michael Grant, distinguished historian and classical scholar, agreed that the themes found in the legend of Jason and the Argonauts have much in common with folktales and myths of other countries. According to Grant:

. . . there are innumerable stories like Jason's, in which the hero is sent on a dangerous journey to get rid of him and, when he arrives at his destination, is confronted with tasks and helped in them by the daughter of the ferocious local ruler; the Norse *Mastermaid* and the Gaelic *Battle of the Birds* are related to the same themes.[9]

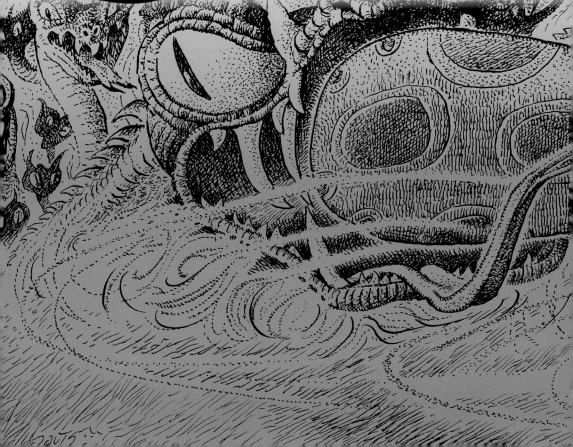

5 The Labors of Heracles

INTRODUCTION

Heracles, the most popular Greek hero, was revered throughout Greece and later, in Rome, where he was known as Hercules. He was not exceptionally intelligent, as was the Athenian hero Theseus (see Chapter 7). Rather, Heracles focused on meeting physical challenges, such as defeating monsters. In fact, his strength was greater than he realized, so that he on occasion killed people unintentionally, actions for which he showed a deep desire to atone. This humility and remorse were part of what endeared him to the Greeks. Heracles showed no hesitation in displaying his feelings, whether joy, anger, disappointment, or sadness. He endured suffering without complaint. After a life filled with many exploits and much suffering, Heracles was taken up to Mount Olympus, home of the gods, where he became divine.

Heracles was the son of Zeus, king of the gods, and Alcmena, granddaughter of the hero Perseus and wife of Amphitryon. Zeus had fallen in love with Alcmena because she was so beautiful. To seduce her, Zeus waited until Amphitryon was away from home. Then he deceived Alcmena by assuming the form of Amphitryon and made her pregnant. When Amphitryon returned, he, too, made love to Alcmena, and she also became pregnant by her husband, so that she was carrying twins.

When Hera found out that Zeus had seduced Alcmena, she was furious with her husband and decided to prevent the baby's birth. When the time came, Zeus announced that a child related to him would be born that day. This child, who was also a descendant of Perseus, would become a king. Zeus meant for the prophecy to apply to Heracles. However, Hera delayed the birth of Heracles by making Alcmena's labor extremely long and difficult. In the meantime, Menippe, who was married to Perseus' son Sthenelus, gave birth to Eurystheus. Zeus' prophecy had come true, although not in the way he had intended. As we shall see, Eurystheus also played an important role in the life of Heracles, especially since Hera became his patron goddess and watched out for him.

After a week in labor, Alcmena gave birth to her twins, Heracles, her divine son, and Iphicles, whom she knew to be Amphitryon's child. From the time of his birth, Heracles' strength and divine heritage were evident. Hera sent a pair of snakes to kill the infant Heracles but he easily strangled the snakes with his bare hands. Later, he quickly learned all the skills a future hero would need, such as chariot driving, wrestling, archery, and playing music.

This myth depicts how Heracles' emotions overwhelmed him at times, causing him to inflict death upon innocent persons. It also describes Heracles' remorse when he had committed such terrible deeds, and his willingness to do penance for his mistakes. In this myth, Heracles must complete twelve seemingly impossible tasks, known as the Labors of Heracles, as a penance for murder.

Featured in the Eleventh Labor of Heracles is the Titan Atlas. The Titans were the twelve children of Uranus, the ruler of the sky, and Gaea, Mother Earth. The Titans, who had human characteristics, ruled the earth for a time, but their reign ended when Zeus and the other Olympian gods defeated the Titans in a war. Zeus punished Atlas for his role in the war by forcing him to hold the heavens on his shoulders. His name came to be associated with Mount Atlas, the mythical continent of Atlantis, and the Atlantic Ocean.

In addition to Heracles, the myth features Megara, his wife, and their children; Hera, queen of the gods; Amphitryon, Heracles' stepfather; the oracle at Delphi; Eurystheus, king of Tiryns and Mycenae; the Nemean Lion; the Cerynean Hind; Artemis, goddess of the hunt, childbirth, and the moon; Apollo, god of music and medicine; the Erymanthian Boar; King Augeas of Elis; the Stymphalian Birds; the Cretan Bull; the Mares of Diomedes; Hippolyta, queen of the Amazons; Geryon, a monster; Helius, god of the sun; the Titan Atlas; the sea-god Nereus; Cerberus, the Hound of Hades; Hades, god of the Underworld; and Hades' queen, Persephone.

The Labors of Heracles

The great hero Heracles had married Megara, the daughter of Creon, king of Thebes. They shared great happiness together with their three children, to whom Heracles showed warm devotion. Perhaps because Heracles was so happy, Hera decided to take further revenge on him. She caused him to become mad, or temporarily insane. While in this fit of madness, he killed Megara and their children.

When Heracles awoke from his madness, he stared at his blood-covered hands. "What has happened?" he asked Amphitryon, his stepfather.

Amphitryon said slowly, "You have killed Megara and your children. Yet you cannot be held responsible for this deed, for the goddess Hera sent a veil of madness over you."

Heracles trembled at the awful thing he had done, showing the guilt he always felt when he had done something wrong. "Even if Hera did cause me to do this, I must still pay the penalty for my actions."

Heracles remained overcome by emotion. He could not rid himself of thoughts of what he considered to be his evil deeds. He felt he deserved punishment. Heracles asked the oracle at Delphi how he might be forgiven for this crime. The oracle told him to serve Eurystheus, king of Tiryns and Mycenae, for twelve years. Eurystheus, who was jealous of Heracles' strength and his growing fame, was cunning and assigned Heracles twelve nearly impossible tasks, which became known as the Twelve Labors of Heracles.

For his first labor, Heracles had to kill a fierce lion who was terrorizing the countryside around Nemea, a village west of Mycenae. The hide of the Nemean Lion could not be penetrated by arrows or weapons of iron or bronze, so Heracles cut himself a sturdy wooden club. He chased the Nemean Lion into its lair, which had an opening at either end. He blocked one opening with gigantic rocks so that the lion could not escape that way. As soon as Heracles entered the lair, the lion charged at him. The mighty hero smashed the beast's head with his club, temporarily stunning it. He seized the creature in his powerful grip and with his bare hands, he choked the lion to death.

Heracles lifted the lion's carcass onto his broad shoulders and returned to the palace of Eurystheus. The sight of the mighty hero filled Eurystheus with fear, and he gave orders that Heracles was not to be allowed to enter the palace. Henceforth, the cowardly king would have a messenger present the next task to Heracles while the hero waited outside the palace. Just to be safe, Eurystheus had also ordered that a massive bronze jar be buried into the ground, so that he could hide inside it whenever he received word that Heracles was near the palace.

Eurystheus wanted nothing to do with the Nemean Lion's carcass, so Heracles decided to keep its hide as a trophy. Heracles broke his knife trying to remove the lion's impenetrable skin, so he used one of the lion's own claws to remove the hide. After that, Heracles always carried the club he had used and wore the lion's skin, and he was frequently portrayed in sculpture and paintings with these objects.

In the Second Labor of Heracles, the hero killed the Lernaean Hydra, a monster with nine heads that lived in the swamps of Lerna near the city of Argos. This story is told in more detail in the next chapter, "The Lernaean Hydra and the Death of Heracles."

Next, Heracles had to capture alive the Cerynean Hind, a doe that had antlers like a male deer. However, these antlers were golden, so the doe was also known as the Golden Hind. It lived on Cerynea, a mountain in Arcadia in the northern Peloponnesus, and was sacred to Artemis, goddess of the hunt, childbirth, and the moon. Heracles had to be careful as he searched for the doe, for harming it in any way would anger the goddess. It took Heracles a full year to capture the deer, but he finally wore it out by chasing it for many months. Carefully, Heracles lifted the hind over his shoulders and started back to the palace of Eurystheus. On the way, he met Artemis and her brother Apollo, god of music, medicine, and prophecy. They were furious with Heracles, for they thought that the Golden Hind was dead. However, Heracles was quick to show them that the animal survived and

Heroes in Greek Mythology Rock!

to explain about the labor he had been assigned. Artemis forgave Heracles, especially because he promised to set the doe free once he had completed his labor, which he did.

The fourth labor was to capture alive the Erymanthian Boar, a savage wild hog that lived on Mount Erymanthus in Arcadia. Heracles chased the boar into deep snowdrifts and captured it alive in nets. When he brought it back to Eurystheus, the king cowered in fear in his bronze jar.

Still, Eurystheus acted unimpressed with Heracles' mighty labors and next sent him out on a particularly dirty and disgusting task—cleaning the Augean Stables in one day. The stables were named after Augeas, king of the area of Elis in the

northwestern Peloponnesus. Augeas owned large herds of cattle, but he had never before had their stables cleaned, so, of course, the stable floors were buried in muck. Augeas promised to reward Heracles with one-tenth of his herds for accomplishing this seemingly impossible task.

Heracles dug new channels for the nearby Alpheus and Peneus rivers, which would divert them right through the Augean Stables. After Heracles dammed their existing channels, the rivers flowed with great speed down their new courses, rushing through the stables. The waters carried away with them all the years of accumulated dung. After his task was completed, Heracles returned the rivers to their original riverbeds. However, once King Augeas learned that Eurystheus had assigned the task of cleaning the stables to Heracles, he refused to keep his promise to pay Heracles for his efforts. Heracles vowed to seek revenge against the king after he finished his labors.

Next Eurystheus ordered Heracles to travel to Arcadia, where the Stymphalian Birds were ravaging the area around Lake Stymphalus. These savage birds had feathers that they shot like arrows and beaks that could pierce armor. Using these weapons, the Stymphalian Birds had killed many people and then eaten their flesh. Hephaestus, the blacksmith of the gods, crafted for Heracles a pair of bronze castanets, or rattles. By shaking the castanets, Heracles made a clanging noise that lured the birds from deep within the forest where they hid. As the screeching birds flew up into the air, Heracles shot them down with his arrows.

The seventh labor was catching alive the Cretan Bull, the father of the Minotaur, a half-bull, half-human monster, that Poseidon, god of the sea, had given to King Minos of Crete, an island in the Aegean Sea. After journeying to Crete, Heracles cornered the bull and seized it by the horns. He carried it to the sea, where he tossed it in the water. He rode the bull across sea and land, back to the palace of Eurystheus. After showing the king that he had captured the massive bull, Heracles set the animal free, and it traveled through the countryside until it ended up in the plain of Marathon, near Athens, where Theseus later caught it.

The next labor was to capture the Mares of Diomedes, a son of Ares, the god of war. Diomedes was the king of a fierce tribe in Thrace, a region northeast of Greece. His mares were not ordinary horses, for they ate human flesh, and they had to be held fast in their stalls by iron chains to keep them from escaping. But Heracles was not afraid of these animals, because he knew of a food that would surely appeal to them: their own master. Heracles tamed the mares by feeding pieces of Diomedes to them, a fitting punishment for the king, because he had taught the mares to enjoy the flesh of humans in the first place. Then Heracles herded the horses to Eurystheus, who set them free and dedicated them to Hera.

Eurystheus next commanded Heracles to fetch the Girdle of Hippolyta, queen of the Amazons, a race of warrior women who lived near the southern shores of the Black Sea. The girdle, a gift of Ares, the god of war, was a belt Hippolyta used to carry her sword. She assured Heracles that he could have the girdle. Unfortunately, Hera again caused trouble. She convinced the Amazons that Heracles was going to capture their queen. The warrior women attacked Heracles, and he strangled Hippolyta, quickly forgetting her friendliness and promise to assist him. Heracles fought off the remaining Amazons and carried off the girdle.

Heracles, for the tenth labor, had to bring to Eurystheus the Cattle of Geryon, a monster with three bodies joined at the waist. Geryon lived on the island of Erythia, which the Greeks believed was at the far western edge of the world. Geryon's herd of cattle was guarded by Eurytion, his gigantic cowherd, and Orthus, a two-headed watchdog.

En route to Erythia, Heracles made his way across the sands of Libya, on the northern coast of Africa, to what is now the eastern entrance to the Strait of Gibraltar, the narrow waterway between the Mediterranean Sea and the Atlantic Ocean. There, on either side of the opening, he supposedly set up two gigantic, peaked

pillars, which are known today as the Rock of Gibraltar and the Rock of Ceuta (in Morocco). The ancient Greeks called these rocks the Pillars of Heracles, and for them, they symbolized the boundary between the known Greek world and the vast unknown.

The desert sands were so hot that Heracles shot one of his arrows at Helius, the god of the sun, in protest. Helius, instead of getting mad at Heracles, admired his courage at showing anger to a god and decided to help him. To make Heracles' journey to Erythia faster and easier, Helius gave Heracles the cup in which the sun sailed in the River of Ocean, which the Greeks believed circled the world. Every night, Helius supposedly used this cup to travel from the western to the eastern horizon for the start of a new day.

When he reached Erythia, Heracles killed Geryon, his two-headed hound, and his giant herdsman. He then herded the cattle into Helius' cup and sailed back to the known world, landing on the coast of Spain. After returning the cup to Helius, Heracles herded the cattle to Eurystheus, who sacrificed them to Hera, his patron goddess.

As if Heracles had not traveled enough, on his next labor he had to go again to the ends of the earth, to the Garden of the Hesperides, to fetch the Golden Apples. The apples represented immortality, or eternal life, and grew on a tree with sparkling golden bark and leaves, which Zeus had given to Hera when they married. The Hesperides, daughters of the Titan Atlas, tended the fruit, and a hundred-headed serpent guarded the tree. The ancient sea-god Nereus knew where the garden was located, and Heracles wrestled with him to force Nereus to tell him the location. Trying desperately to escape Heracles' grasp, Nereus changed himself into flames, a lion, a serpent, a stream of water, and a fierce boar. Finally, Nereus realized that Heracles' grasp was too powerful to escape, and he revealed to the hero that the garden was near the western edge of the world near where Atlas held up the heavens on his shoulders.

When Heracles arrived at the garden, he convinced Atlas to fetch the apples. The Hesperides were his daughters, so Atlas stood a better chance of safely accomplishing the task. While Atlas was gone, Heracles held up the sky for him. However, Atlas so enjoyed his freedom that when he returned from the garden, he refused to take back the burden of holding up the sky. So Heracles asked Atlas to hold the sky just until Heracles could make a pad for his shoulders. Once Atlas took the sky back onto his shoulders, Heracles escaped with the Golden Apples. After Heracles gave them to Eurystheus, the goddess Athena returned them to the garden.

The last labor was the one that Heracles deemed his most difficult—a journey to the Underworld, the land of the dead, where the god Hades ruled. Heracles had to face the powers of death and bring back Cerberus, the three-headed Hound of Hades. Cerberus, who had a dragon's tail, ate anyone who tried to leave Hades.

To reach Hades, Heracles traveled to Taenarum, at the southern edge of the Peloponnesus near Sparta, where caves led to the entrance to the Underworld. As Heracles bravely entered the Underworld, all the shades, or ghosts of the dead, fled in fear. When he met Hades, ruler of the Underworld, and his lovely queen, Persephone, Heracles explained his task. Hades agreed that Heracles could take the hound, provided he did not use any weapons to capture it. Heracles, wrapped in his lion skin and protected by his breastplate, grabbed Cerberus in a fierce grip. While Cerberus thrashed, trying to escape, Heracles maintained his hold, even though the hound's dragon tail bit him. After putting a chain around the neck of the growling hound, Heracles dragged it up to the world of the living. Of course, once Eurystheus saw the snarling beast, he wanted to have nothing to do with it, so Heracles returned Cerberus to Hades.

Zeus' mighty son had well and faithfully completed all of his Labors. He had truly earned the right to immortality.

QUESTIONS AND ANSWERS

Q: *Why did Heracles kill his family?*

A: Hera, queen of the gods, caused him to go mad.

Q: *What did Heracles have to do in order to be forgiven for killing his wife and children?*

A: He had to perform twelve labors for King Eurystheus of Tiryns and Mycenae.

Q: *Why did Heracles have to be careful when hunting the Cerynean Hind?*

A: The hind was sacred to Artemis, goddess of the hunt, childbirth, and the moon. Harming it in any way would anger the goddess.

Q: *What was the Erymanthian Boar?*

A: It was a savage wild hog that lived on Mount Erymanthus.

Q: *How did Heracles clean out the Augean Stables?*

A: He diverted the path of two rivers so that they flowed through the stables and cleaned out the years of accumulated dung.

Q: *Describe the Stymphalian Birds. How did Heracles conquer them?*

A: They had feathers that they shot like arrows and beaks that could pierce armor. They killed people and ate their flesh. Heracles defeated them by creating deafening noise with castanets, which drove the birds out of their forest hiding place. He then shot the birds with arrows.

Q: *What was the Cretan Bull?*

A: It was the father of the monstrous Minotaur.

Q: *What did Heracles do with the Mares of Diomedes?*

A: He fed them the flesh of Diomedes, who had taught them to enjoy human flesh.

Q: *What was the prize that Heracles took from Hippolyta?*

A: He captured her girdle, a belt that she used to carry her sword. This girdle had been a gift of Ares, god of war.

Q: *Who was Geryon?*

A: He was a monster with three bodies joined at the waist that Heracles killed for his tenth labor.

Q: *What are the Pillars of Heracles and what did they symbolize to the ancient Greeks?*

A: They are two large rock pillars that Heracles set up on either side of the Strait of Gibraltar. They represented the boundary between the known and unknown worlds.

Q: *Why did Helius, god of the sun, decide to help Heracles?*

A: He admired Heracles' courage at showing anger to a god.

Q: *Atlas agreed to fetch the Golden Apples for Heracles if he would take over holding the sky on his shoulders for Atlas. When Atlas returned with the fruit, how did Heracles trick Atlas into taking back the burden of holding the heavens on his shoulders?*

A: Heracles said he needed to make a pad for his shoulders. Once Atlas took the sky back on his shoulders, Heracles escaped with the Golden Apples.

Q: *Which labor did Heracles say was his most difficult and why?*

A: Heracles considered the journey to the Underworld to fetch Cerberus, the Hound of Hades, to be the hardest because he had to face the powers of death.

EXPERT COMMENTARY

Because of the legendary deeds of Heracles, famous Greek scholar Edith Hamilton wrote of him that:

> The greatest hero of Greece was Hercules [sic]. He was a personage of quite another order from the great hero of Athens, Theseus. He was what all Greece except Athens most admired. The Athenians were different from the other Greeks and their hero therefore was different. Theseus was, of course, bravest of the brave as all heroes are, but unlike other heroes he was compassionate as he was brave and a man of great intellect as well as great bodily strength. It was natural that the Athenians should have such a hero because they valued thought and ideas as no other part of the country did. In Theseus their ideal was embodied. But Hercules [sic] embodied what the rest of Greece most valued. His qualities were those the Greeks in general honored and admired. Except for unflinching courage, they were not those that distinguished Theseus.[1]

Lucilla Burn, a curator in the department of Greek and Roman antiquities at the British Museum, provided additional support for this characterization of Heracles:

> Herakles [sic] was the Greek Superman, and many of the stories of his deeds are simply gripping tales of superhuman achievements and fabulous monsters. At the same time Herakles [sic], like Odysseus, stands for the average man, and his adventures are exaggerated parables of human experience. Quick-tempered, not terribly bright, fond of wine, food and women . . ., he was an eminently sympathetic figure; and on the whole his example was to be emulated, for he destroyed evil and championed good, rising above all the blows that fortune showered on him. Above all, he offered some hope of defeating man's ultimate and crucial challenge, death.[2]

Burn added: "In adult life the adventures of Herakles [sic] were both more extensive and more spectacular than those of any other hero. Throughout antiquity he was hugely popular, the subject of numerous stories and countless works of art."[3]

The ancient Greeks believed that Heracles was human before he became immortal. According to professors Mark P. O. Morford and Robert J. Lenardon:

> . . . the ambiguity of Heracles' status as man and god is evident. That he was a man before he became a god is shown by his name (which means "glory of Hera"), "since Greek gods do not form their names from compounds of other gods' names."[4]

The myths of Heracles are so old that they may have roots in other cultures, according to Professor Barry B. Powell:

> Some would trace the story of Heracles' birth to the Egyptian tradition, which is portrayed in reliefs showing sexual union between god and queen in Egyptian temples. A charming poem inscribed on the funerary monument of Queen Hatshepsut (1490—1468 B.C.) accompanies such a relief, telling of Amun's appearance to Ahmes, wife of Tuthmosis I, to beget the divine child Hatshepsut. Thoth, god of writing and magic, leads Amun to the queen's chamber.[5]

Although the exact origins of the myth of Heracles are unclear, classical scholars Mark P. O. Morford and Robert J. Lenardon noted that there was a "nearly unanimous view of the ancients that Heracles the man became a god."[6]

6

The Lernaean Hydra and the Death of Heracles

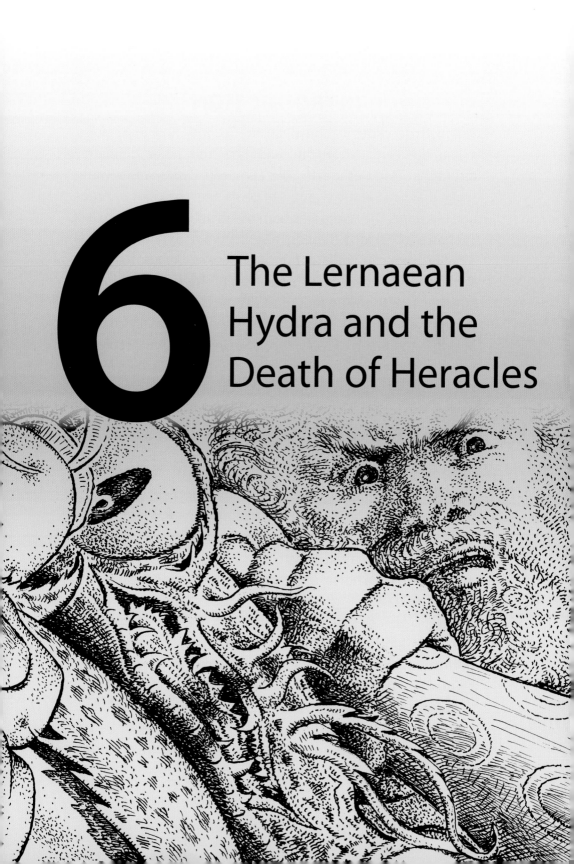

INTRODUCTION

This myth describes in more detail the Second Labor of Heracles, killing the Lernaean Hydra, and how this labor ultimately resulted in Heracles' death. The Lernaean Hydra was a water snake that lived in the swamps of Lerna near the cities of Argos and Mycenae. The Hydra was born of the union of the monsters Typhon and Echidna. Typhon, also known as Typhoeus, was a gigantic monster with a hundred snakes' heads for arms. Typhon tried to overthrow Zeus, king of the gods, by chasing after him and throwing mountains at the mighty god. But Zeus hurled the mountains right back at Typhon and finally crushed him with the island of Sicily. Typhon's breath is supposedly the cause of the smoke and flames belching from Sicily's Mount Etna. Echidna was a half-nymph, half-snake creature who also gave birth to the Crommyon Sow, a monster that the hero Theseus killed, and the Nemean Lion, that featured in the first of the Twelve Labors of Heracles.

Other mythical creatures make this myth an interesting one. Heracles fights a battle with the river god Acheloüs, who, like many of the gods, is able to transform himself into a variety of creatures. In this myth, he takes on the form of a mighty boar. A centaur, a creature with the head and torso of a human and the body of a horse, plays an important part in the ultimate death of Heracles.

Iolaüs, Heracles' nephew, assists him in this myth. He was the son of Iphicles, Heracles' mortal brother, born of the union of Alcmena, Heracles' mother, and Amphitryon, Heracles' stepfather. The Greeks believe he was the first settler of Sardinia, an island in the Mediterranean off the coast of Italy.

The archer Philoctetes lit Heracles' funeral pyre, or bed of materials piled to burn a body at a funeral. In gratitude,

Heracles gave Philoctetes his bow and arrows before he died. Philoctetes used these objects during the Trojan War, firing the arrow that killed Paris, the Trojan who started the war by kidnaping Helen, the wife of King Menelaus of Sparta.

This myth also includes an explanation of the origin of a constellation, or group of stars. When ancient Greek mapmakers and astronomers looked up into the skies, they tried to make sense of the thousands of twinkling stars. They noticed that many of the stars were organized into groups or patterns. The Greeks believed that the gods had organized the stars into these patterns to immortalize mythological monsters as well as humans. They observed that the sun passed through twelve of the constellations, which became the signs of the Zodiac. As Heracles fought against the Lernaean Hydra, a giant crab also crawled out of the Lernaean Swamp and attacked Heracles. Although the crab did not defeat Heracles, Hera, queen of the gods, rewarded the crab for its efforts and transformed it into one of the signs of the Zodiac, the constellation Cancer, which means crab.

By rewarding the crab for its efforts, Hera continued to demonstrate her ill feelings toward Heracles, who represented a larger-than-life reminder that Hera's husband Zeus, king of the gods, had often been unfaithful to her. However, by the end of the myth, Zeus convinced Hera to reconcile with Heracles.

The Lernaean Hydra and the Death of Heracles

The Second Labor of Heracles was to kill the Lernaean Hydra, which had been ravaging the countryside, destroying fields and killing cattle. This nine-headed water serpent lived in the murky swamps of Lerna, southeast of Mycenae. Although eight of the serpent's heads were mortal, one in the center was immortal. Together with his nephew Iolaüs and armed with his sword, bow, arrows, and club, Heracles drove in a chariot to the swamp, ready to do battle with the monster.

Heracles quickly flushed the Hydra from its swampy lair by shooting flaming arrows at it. Heracles moved in for the kill, but the monster wrapped itself tightly around his foot. Heracles smashed at the Hydra's heads with his club, but this weapon proved useless. Then, Heracles drew his sword and slashed at the serpent's heads. But this made the situation even more threatening, for every time Heracles successfully cut off one of the Hydra's heads, two others grew back in its place.

To make matters worse, a giant crab scuttled out from the depths of the swamp and bit fiercely at Heracles' trapped foot. Hera watched in glee from Mount Olympus, for she took great pleasure in anything that made Heracles' life more difficult. To her, he was a living reminder of her husband Zeus' many relationships with other women. But then Heracles

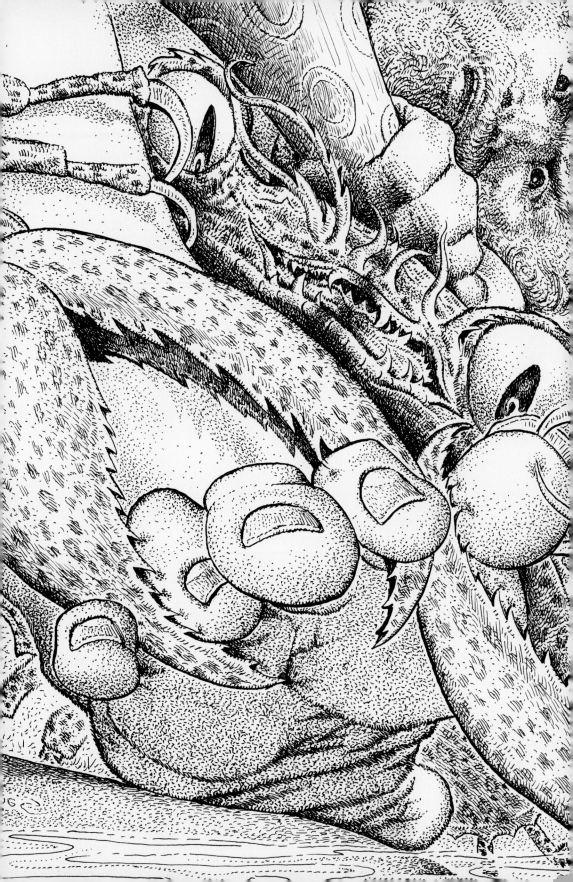

smashed the crab with his club. Even though the monster had not been able to stop Heracles from continuing his attack upon the Hydra, the queen of the gods rewarded the crab by placing it eternally among the heavens as the constellation Cancer.

Although Heracles had done away with the crab, he called out to his nephew to help him kill the Hydra. Heracles instructed Iolaüs to cut torches from the nearby forest and set them on fire. Each time Heracles cut off one of the monster's mortal heads, Iolaüs moved in with a blazing torch and held it to the stump to sear it before any new heads could start to grow. Finally, all the mortal heads were destroyed. Then Heracles cut off the immortal one and buried it underneath a huge rock.

In a fury, Heracles tore open the monster's body and dipped his arrow points into the bile, or venomous liquid inside the body cavity. From that day forward, these arrows caused incurable wounds to their victims. In fact, years later, Heracles himself became a victim of the poisonous bile, which is the next part of our story.

After he had completed his twelve labors as well as many other adventures, Heracles decided to seek a new bride. When Heracles was in the Underworld on his twelfth labor, he encountered the ghost of Meleager, the leader of the Calydonian Boar Hunt. Meleager told him about his sister Deïanira, whom Meleager thought would make Heracles a wonderful wife. And so Heracles decided to go to Calydon to seek the hand of Meleager's sister in marriage.

Unfortunately, Acheloüs, a river god who often took on other forms, also wanted to marry Deïanira. At times, Acheloüs transformed himself into a slippery snake, a hissing dragon, or a ferocious wild boar, none of which appealed to a beautiful young woman. But Acheloüs was, after all, a god, so no mortal suitors had the courage to ask for Deïanira's hand. Heracles, as befitted a great hero, had no such qualms, for he was supremely confident in his physical ability to meet all trials. He challenged the river god to a wrestling match, with the winner to wed Deïanira. Acheloüs transformed himself into a wild boar and charged Heracles, snorting and wildly tossing his horned head from side to side. But Heracles would not allow the boar to gore him. He grabbed the boar by the horns and threw him to the ground, breaking one of his horns in the process. The river god acknowledged defeat and slunk back into his river, while Heracles claimed the hand of Deïanira in marriage.

Heracles set off with his bride to Trachis, a city northeast of Calydon. On the way there, the couple had to cross the river Evenus. The centaur Nessus ferried travelers across the river for a small fee, and he offered to carry Deïanira. While the lovely young woman rode on the centaur's back, Heracles began to swim across the river. In the center of the stream, however, Nessus tried to seduce Deïanira. As soon as Heracles heard her cries for help, he drew an arrow from his quiver, and fired the arrow with his massive bow. As soon as the arrow point pierced the hide of the centaur, it began to fill his bloodstream with the poison of the Lernaean Hydra. Nessus dragged himself to shore and decided to take revenge on Heracles for shooting him. Just before he died, Nessus told Deïanira to save some of his blood for a love potion. He said that it would keep Heracles from loving another woman more than he loved Deïanira.

While staying at Trachis, Heracles went on a military campaign and captured a princess, Iole, as a war prize. On his way back to Trachis, Heracles stopped by the sea to perform a sacrifice to Zeus in thanks for his victory in war. Near the wave-washed cliffs, he dedicated a sacred altar to the king of the gods. Then he sent a messenger named Lichas to Trachis to bring back a special shirt that Heracles always used in such religious rites. Deïanira feared that Heracles had fallen in love with Iole and, remembering the advice of the centaur Nessus, rubbed Heracles' shirt in the love potion.

Heracles put on the shirt and began his sacrifices, offering up a dozen perfect bulls to Zeus, his father. But then the fires of the sacrificial altar blazed up, fed by the blood of the bulls, and joined with the heat of the burning firewood. Heracles broke out into a sweat, which caused his shirt to cling to his skin. Agonizing, cramping pain consumed his body. The centaur had tricked Deïanira, for his blood was not a love potion. It was poison, tainted by the bile of the Lernaean Hydra. When Deïanira heard what had happened, she realized that the love potion had caused Heracles tremendous pain and that she was responsible, even though she did not intend to cause Heracles such pain. She immediately went out and hanged herself.

With raging pain still coursing through his body, Heracles seized Lichas by an ankle and smashed the messenger against a reef in the nearby sea. Bystanders were stunned as the very lifeblood of Lichas drained from his body. But none would think of blaming Heracles for his action, for he clearly was in such enormous pain. Still, no one had the courage to approach Heracles, for they were afraid of his awesome power and did not want to suffer the same fate as Lichas. Finally, Heracles called out to his son, Hyllus.

"My dear Son," he moaned. "Carry me to where none can see my pain."

"Father," Hyllus answered, "I shall carry you far across the water, far from this place. I will not let you die here."

Hyllus carried his father to Mount Oeta near Trachis. There he gathered the family and friends of Heracles to set up a massive funeral pyre. Heracles dragged himself atop the pyre, writhing in agony and close to death. Still, none of his family, friends, or servants would dare move close to Heracles and light the funeral pyre, for none could forget how Heracles' pain had caused the death of Lichas. Heracles begged for someone to end his agony by lighting the pyre, so Philoctetes, who later fought for the Greeks in the Trojan War, finally stepped forward to do it. A grateful Heracles, deeply in pain, gave Philoctetes his bow and arrows.

A cloud descended from the heavens, obscuring Heracles from view. The flames of the pyre blazed up and thunder rumbled. When the ashes of Heracles had finally cooled on the pyre, no trace of his bones were found. This symbolized Heracles' transformation from mortal to divine, for he had been raised up to Olympus, home of the gods.

In a procession with the host of Olympian gods, Heracles passed through the halls of Zeus, mighty king of the gods. Before the throne of Zeus, Heracles bowed low. Zeus turned to Hera, his wife and queen.

"Hera, my queen, the time has come to end your terrible persecution of Heracles. I know that I have given you much cause for anger, but Heracles is blameless," Zeus said.

Hera addressed Heracles. "You have suffered much and with great courage. I promise to cease my jealousy and anger against you and replace it with love. As a token of my promise, take the hand of Hebe, my daughter, in marriage."

And so, loved and honored by the gods, Heracles married Hebe, whose name means "youth." Now, like Hebe, Heracles would be eternally youthful and live forever in happiness among the immortal gods.

QUESTIONS AND ANSWERS

Q: *What happened when Heracles cut off one of the Hydra's mortal heads?*

A: Two grew back in its place.

Q: *What other creature attacked Heracles?*

A: A gigantic crab bit Heracles' foot.

Q: *What was the crab's fate and what did it symbolize?*

A: Heracles destroyed the crab with his club. However, Hera was glad that the crab had attacked Heracles, because to her, Heracles represented one of Zeus' many relationships with other women. Hera rewarded the crab by putting it up in the sky as the constellation Cancer, meaning crab.

Q: *After Heracles killed the Hydra, what did he do with his arrow points? How did this affect the arrows?*

A: Heracles dipped his arrow points into the Hydra's bile. After that, the arrow points caused incurable wounds.

Q: *How did Heracles win the hand of Deïanira and how did this exhibit his heroic qualities?*

A: Heracles defeated Acheloüs in a wrestling match. He was not afraid to challenge Acheloüs to this fight, even though other mortals were afraid to face him because he was divine.

Q: *Who was Nessus?*

A: He was a centaur who ferried travelers across the River Evenus.

Q: *What did Nessus do to Deïanira?*

A: He tried to seduce her when he carried her across the river.

Q: *How did Heracles react when he heard Deïanira's cry for help?*

A: He shot Nessus with one of his poisoned arrows.

Q: *How did Nessus take revenge on Heracles for killing him?*

A: Before he died, Nessus told Deïanira to keep some of his blood for a love potion that would keep Heracles from loving another woman more than he loved Deïanira.

Q: *Who was Iole and what concern did Deïanira have about her?*

A: She was a princess whom Heracles captured as a prize of war. Deïanira thought that Heracles had fallen in love with Iole.

Q: *After Heracles was victorious in war, he set up a sacred altar to offer sacrifices of thanks to Zeus. What object did he require to complete his sacrificial offerings and how did he obtain it?*

A: He sent a messenger, Lichas, to Trachis to get the special shirt that he used in such religious rites.

Q: *What did Deïanira do to the shirt before she gave it to the messenger?*

A: She rubbed it in the love potion she had gotten from the centaur Nessus.

Q: *What was wrong with the love potion and how did it affect Heracles' shirt?*

A: The potion was actually poison, tainted by the bile of the Lernaean Hydra. When Heracles put on the shirt, the flames of the sacrificial fires caused Heracles to sweat. The sweat made the shirt stick to Heracles' body, and it activated the poison. The poison filled Heracles' body with intense pain.

Q: *What terrible action did Heracles commit while writhing in agony from the pain caused by the poison?*

A: He grabbed Lichas by the ankle and smashed him down with such force that the messenger died.

Q: *What did Deïanira do when she learned how her love potion had affected Heracles?*

A: Even though she had been unaware of how terribly the potion would affect Heracles, she assumed responsibility for the pain it had caused and killed herself.

Q: *How did Hyllus help his father, Heracles?*

A: He carried him to Mount Oeta and gathered friends and relatives to build a funeral pyre for Heracles.

Q: *What brave action did Philoctetes perform and how was he rewarded?*

A: Everyone was afraid to light the funeral pyre, for they remembered how Heracles' pain had caused him to lash out at Lichas and kill him. Philoctetes stepped forward to light the pyre and a grateful Heracles gave him his bow and arrows.

Q: *After the flames on the funeral pyre had burned out, what remained and what did this symbolize?*

A: Only Heracles' ashes remained, not his bones, which symbolized his ascension to Olympus and his transformation to an immortal god.

Q: *When Heracles reached Olympus, how did Hera react to him?*

A: Zeus convinced her to cease her tormenting of Heracles, and she welcomed him with love, offering her daughter, Hebe, to Heracles in marriage.

Q: *What does Hebe's name mean and what does this symbolize?*

A: Her name means "youth" and represents Heracles' immortality and his acceptance by the gods.

EXPERT COMMENTARY

The Labors of Heracles were the theme of carvings on the temple of Zeus at Olympia, in the western Peloponnesus. The sculptures contain all twelve of the Labors of Heracles. However, the order of the labors took time to develop, according to classics professors Mark P. O. Morford and Robert J. Lenardon:

> . . . there is, however, great confusion over the chronology of Heracles' legends. Euripides in his *Heracles* puts the murder of Megara and her children after the Labors. Sophocles in his *Trachiniae* has Heracles marry his second wife Deïanira before the Labors, whereas Apollodorus places the marriage after them. All are agreed that for a number of years Heracles served Eurystheus.[1]

Eurystheus, whom Heracles served for his twelve labors, was not satisfied with the death of the hero, according to Professor Barry B. Powell:

> When Heracles died, Eurystheus was determined to kill the many sons, fathered on many women, whom Heracles had left behind, called the Heraclids. They fled, first to Trachis, then to Athens, where they took refuge at the Altar of Mercy. The Athenians bravely refused to surrender the refugees, took up arms, and defeated Eurystheus and killed five of his sons, although the king himself escaped in a chariot. Hyllus gave chase and ran him down near the rocks where Theseus had killed Sciron. He cut off Eurystheus' head and brought it to Alcmena, who, laughingly, poked out its eyes with large bronze pins. . . .
>
> The classical Greeks identified the legendary return of the Heraclids with the Dorian invasion that caused the collapse of the Mycenaean world about 1200 B.C. The Dorians of the Peloponnesus always claimed to be direct descendants of Heracles and made of Heracles their special hero. But Heracles was never a local or tribal hero: At all times he belonged to all the Greeks.[2]

The ancient Greeks believed that with Heracles' death, he and Hera reconciled and Heracles assumed immortality. Pindar (518–438 B.C.), who was considered the greatest lyric poet in Greek literature, wrote odes, or poems in honor of the victors at ancient Greece's greatest national games. In the *Isthmian Odes*, Pindar described Heracles' ascension to Olympus and his reconciliation with Hera:

> To Olympus went Alcmena's son, when he had explored every land and the cliff-girt levels of the foaming sea, to tame the straits for seafarers. Now beside Zeus he enjoys a perfect happiness; he is loved and honored by the immortals; Hebe is his wife, and he is lord of a golden palace, the husband of Hera's daughter.[3]

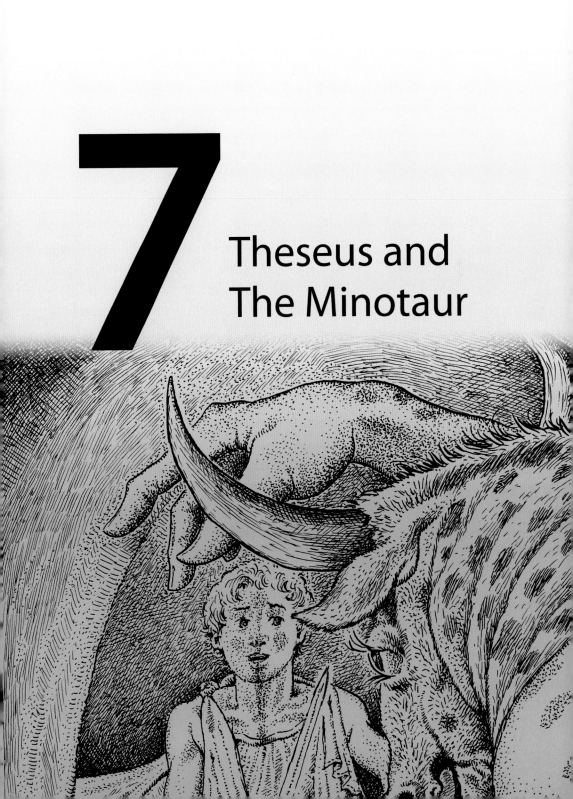

7

Theseus and
The Minotaur

INTRODUCTION

Some Greek myths had a basis in historical fact and concerned real people, usually kings or other royal personages, as well as heroes who had made important names for themselves in ages long past. Gradually, as these historical tales were retold, the line between myth and history became blurred. This was the case with the story about Theseus and the Minotaur. Although Theseus was featured in many mythological tales about his bravery and heroic deeds, he also became an important political symbol for Athens of the early fifth century B.C. Theseus was a popular subject of both Greek and Roman writers, including the poet Ovid, who lived from about 43 B.C. to A.D. 17. Theseus was also featured in the plays of two of Athen's great playwrights, Euripides and Sophocles. Many of the legends about Theseus have as their source the *Life of Theseus* by Plutarch (A.D. 46?–120), a Greek essayist and biographer. Plutarch presented "myth as history."[1] Since Plutarch was interested in "the moral excellence (or defects) of the people whose biographies he wrote, the relationship between myth and historical fact is not as distant as it would be for a modern biographer."[2]

Theseus became the great national hero of Attica, the region where Athens was located, and Athens came to be the focus of the legends about him. He was also linked with Troezen, where he was born, and with Marathon, a plain near Athens. One of the tales about Theseus described how he killed a bull that was causing great destruction in Marathon. (The basis for the modern marathon race came later, when in 490 B.C., the Greeks defeated the Persians in the Battle of Marathon. According to legend, an Athenian messenger ran from

Marathon to Athens, a distance of about 25 miles, to announce the Greek victory. Running such a long distance became known as a marathon.)

The myth of Theseus and the Minotaur, which follows, begins just prior to the birth of Theseus. His father was King Aegeus of Athens and his mother was Aethra, the daughter of the king of Troezen. Before Aegeus left Troezen to return to Athens, he hid a sword and sandals under a gigantic stone. When Theseus was old enough, he was to try to roll away the stone and bring the hidden objects to Athens, where his father would recognize Theseus as his son and heir. In myths throughout the world, a sword buried in or under a rock often symbolized a seemingly unattainable goal set before a hero or royal personage and also represented his royal lineage. Whoever could pull the sword from the rock or move the rock away to recover the sword clearly had heroic, noble qualities. For example, King Arthur, a medieval king of the Britons, became king by extracting his sword, Excalibur, from the stone that held it fast.

The tasks that Theseus accomplished on his journey from Troezen to Athens seemed to have been aimed at rivaling those of the great hero Heracles.[3] Most likely, they were explored in more detail in an epic poem that no longer exists. Theseus idolized Heracles, who was his second cousin (both were descended from the hero Pelops, king of Elis).

Another important location in the myth is the island of Crete, located across the Mediterranean Sea south of Athens. Crete was an important sea power from about 2000–1400 B.C. Minos was the legendary ruler of Cnossus, the main city on Crete, where the bull was an important religious symbol representing fertility. Minos refused to sacrifice a magnificent bull that Poseidon had sent as proof of Minos' kingship.

Poseidon punished Minos by making the king's wife, Pasiphaë, fall hopelessly in love with the bull, and she eventually gave birth to the Minotaur, a man-eating monster with the head of a bull and body of a man. Minos ordered Daedalus, a master architect, to build a maze capable of keeping this monster captive. Daedalus created a series of twistings and turnings known as the Labyrinth. Today, intricate mazes are still known as labyrinths. The term is also applied to a garden maze formed by paths separated by high hedges, or to any complex situation.

In this myth, a variation of human sacrifice is an important part of the story. King Minos of Crete exacted a tribute on the king and the people of Athens in compensation for their murder of his son. (A tribute is a payment paid by one ruler to another to acknowledge submission.) Every nine years, the Athenians had to pay this tribute in the form of humans, specifically seven young men and seven young women, who were to be sacrificed to the Minotaur. It is possible that this legend may have had actual basis in fact, reflecting a time when the Minoan civilization controlled Athens.[4]

Besides Theseus and his parents, Aegeus and Aethra, the myth features many other characters. On the way from Troezen to Athens, Theseus encounters menacing monsters, robbers, and bandits. Upon reaching Athens, Theseus meets Medea, a sorceress, and her son, Medus, in his father's palace. Other characters include Pallas, the brother of Aegeus, and his fifty sons; the Bull of Marathon; King Minos of Crete and his daughter, Ariadne; seven Athenian maidens and seven youths; Daedalus, the inventor of the Labyrinth; a Cretan wrestler; one of Ariadne's servants; the dreaded Minotaur, and Dionysus, god of wine, music, and dancing.

Theseus and the Minotaur

Theseus was the son of King Aegeus of Athens and Aethra, daughter of King Pittheus of Troezen, a city at the northeastern tip of the Peloponnesus. Theseus grew up in Troezen, where he lived with his mother. His father went back to Athens before Theseus was born, but first he hid a sword and a pair of sandals in a hollow under a huge stone.

Aegeus told Aethra, "When Theseus is strong enough to roll away the stone, have him bring the sword and sandals to Athens."

"For what purpose?" Aethra asked.

"Then I will recognize Theseus as my son and heir. For if he is strong enough to move away this stone, he surely will have the qualities of a hero and king."

From the time he was small, Theseus had already showed heroic characteristics. Once, his cousin Heracles, whom Theseus greatly admired, came to visit. Heracles strode into the palace wearing the lion skin he had skinned from the Nemean Lion (see Chapter 5). The other children ran screaming, thinking that a real lion had snuck into the palace. But Theseus showed his bravery by attacking the skin with a small sword.

By the time Theseus was sixteen, he had already grown to be extremely strong. His mother, Aethra, deemed that he was powerful enough to roll away the mighty stone, so she told him about the tokens that Aegeus had hidden underneath it. With the merest touch, Theseus was able to roll away the stone and recover the sword and the sandals.

Immediately, Theseus planned how he would journey to Athens. His mother begged him to go by sea, which would be the fastest and safest way to travel, for there were many monsters and bandits who plagued the overland route. However, rather than travel by ship, Theseus decided to go by land. Such a dangerous route would undoubtedly give Theseus an opportunity to duplicate feats of heroism and bravery such as those accomplished by Heracles. Completing a difficult overland journey would also clearly show that Theseus was the son of a king.

On the road from Troezen to Athens, Theseus encountered a number of menacing monsters, robbers, and bandits, who had made it their habit to prey on innocent passersby as these people made their way from Troezen to Athens. At Epidaurus, a city in the northeastern Peloponnesus, Theseus encountered Periphetes, nicknamed "Clubber." This bandit, a son of Hephaestus, the artisan god and god of blacksmiths, liked to smash travelers over the head with his iron club. Theseus killed him by smashing the skull of Periphetes–with the bandit's own club.

At the Isthmus of Corinth, the narrow strip of land connecting central Greece with the Peloponnesus, Theseus killed the robber Sinis, who was nicknamed "Pinebender." It was Sinis' habit, after robbing a victim, to tie the traveler to two bent pine trees. Then, Sinis would let go of the trees so that they would spring forward and tear the victim in half. Theseus felt that Sinis deserved to be killed in the same fashion he had chosen to administer to his victims.

Theseus headed north to the village of Crommyon, where he used his sword and spear to slay the Sow of Crommyon. No longer would this man-eating boar terrorize the village.

The bandit Sciron blocked a pathway along the sea cliffs so that travelers could not pass by. He forced them to bend down to wash his feet and then kicked them into the sea, where a gigantic sea turtle ate them. Theseus made Sciron wash his feet, and then Theseus kicked him down the steep, rocky slope to the waiting, hungry sea turtle.

Near Athens, Theseus encountered Cercyon, who wrestled travelers to death. Cercyon met his match in Theseus, who wrestled with him and crushed him to death.

Procrustes, the "Stretcher," killed travelers by forcing them to lie on a bed. If they were too short to fit the bed, he pounded them with a hammer until they fit. If they were too long, he sawed off their feet and hands. Theseus killed Procrustes in the same way.

When Theseus arrived in Athens, the people welcomed him warmly, having heard of the mighty deeds he had accomplished. At first, Aegeus was unaware that Theseus was his son. He feared that because Theseus was so popular with the people, they might wish to make the young man king. Aegeus was under the spell of the sorceress Medea, the same witch who had been involved with Jason, the leader of the Argonauts. She had married Aegeus soon after Theseus was born. Medea recognized Theseus right away. She wanted Medus, her own son by Aegeus, to inherit the throne, so Medea offered Theseus a cup filled with poison. Theseus refused to drink it and drew his sword. Aegeus recognized the sword as the one he had buried in Troezen. Aegeus knocked away the cup of poison and hugged Theseus to his chest. Soon after, Aegeus proclaimed Theseus as his son and heir to the throne and banished Medea and Medus to Asia.

Pallas, Aegeus' brother, was jealous of Theseus and angry at Aegeus for naming Theseus as his heir. Pallas and his fifty sons rebelled against Aegeus and Theseus. After Theseus killed many of the rebels, Pallas and his surviving sons fled Athens.

For his next adventure, Theseus caught the Bull of Marathon. Heracles had brought the bull from the island of Crete and released it on the mainland. The beast had wandered to the plain of Marathon, near Athens, where it had caused great destruction. Theseus captured the bull and led it back to Athens. There he gave it to King Aegeus, who sacrificed the bull to the god Apollo.

Aegeus then told Theseus about a terrible tribute, or type of sacrifice, that the city of Athens had to pay to Minos, the ruler of Cnossus, the principal city of the island of Crete. Many years before, the son of Minos had been killed by Athenians while on a visit to Athens. Every nine years after that, Minos demanded that Athens send a tribute of seven young women and seven young men. They were sacrificed to the Minotaur, a horrid monster who was half man, half bull.

"My Son," said Aegeus, "the Minotaur lives in the Labyrinth, a confusing and complicated maze. Our poor young people are put inside this maze, where they are hunted down and eaten by this horrible monster before they can find their way out of the maze."

"A maze, Father? Surely no maze could be so complicated," Theseus said.

Aegeus answered, "It was designed by the great inventor Daedalus. Not a single Athenian has ever returned alive from the maze."

"Father, I must be one of the next fourteen who go to Crete to be sacrificed," said Theseus. "When I am inside the Labyrinth, I will slay the Minotaur, and Athens will be free forever from the burden of this sacrifice."

Aegeus twisted his hands together in anguish. "No, my Son. Now that you have been restored to me, I do not wish to lose you. You must stay safe, so that one day, you can succeed me as the ruler of our people."

"Father, I have a higher duty. I must make every effort to save our young people," Theseus said.

So Aegeus reluctantly agreed that Theseus could go, for he recognized the importance of his son setting a heroic example for the people of Athens. "You may go, Theseus, but you must promise me this: We will send our ship off to the south, across the Mediterranean, to the island of Crete with black sails to show our sadness. If you succeed in killing the Minotaur, you must change the sails to white ones. Then, as soon as the ship enters our harbor, I will know your fate."

When Theseus and the thirteen other young Athenians arrived in Crete, they were first paraded before the citizens and then brought to the palace of the king, where Minos sat on a low throne in a magnificent chamber of red. Theseus, as befitted a hero and a king's son, looked upon Minos without fear. Next to Minos stood his daughter, Ariadne, who was attired in a dress of gleaming fabric that was tight at the waist, very different than the flowing garments worn by the Greek maidens. Ariadne's hair fell to her shoulders in waves, and, instead of sandals, she wore high shoes that shone like glass. As soon as she looked upon Theseus, she fell in love with him.

Now King Minos had heard of the mighty deeds of Theseus, so he asked him to compete in the annual athletic games that the Cretans were holding at that time. He faced a boastful wrestler that none of the other competitors had been able to defeat. The Cretan wrestler was very strong and skillful, but Theseus was mightier still. He bent the wrestler backward and forced him to the ground. Ariadne knew that, with his great physical strength, he had a chance to slay the Minotaur. But the twistings and turnings of the Labyrinth were so devious that Theseus would never be able to find his way in and out of the maze by himself. Ariadne sought out Daedalus, the inventor who had designed the maze, and he told her how to find the center.

That night was to be the last one before the Athenian youths were to be put in the Labyrinth. Each of them was led away to a small sleeping chamber in the palace, from which they would have no chance to escape, for there were many guards about. Late in the evening, Ariadne sent a trusted servant to bring Theseus to her. She smiled at Theseus as she spoke, saying, "I am Ariadne, daughter of King Minos. I know a way to save you from the Minotaur."

"I must save not only myself, but also all of the young men and women who have come with me to Athens to serve as tribute," answered Theseus. "Will your knowledge help me to do this?"

Ariadne replied, "Yes. I can show you a way to find the Minotaur. Then you must slay it and lead the others out of the maze using the trick that I will tell you."

Theseus knew he could rely on his physical skills and his bravery to slay the Minotaur once he found him. "Don't keep me in suspense any longer, Princess. What is this clue that you promise?"

Ariadne told Theseus the secret of locating the center of the maze, which she had learned from Daedalus. She also gave Theseus a ball of thread that he could use to trace his way back out of the Labyrinth. "Tie one end of this ball of thread to the gate at the entrance of the Labyrinth. Carefully unravel the thread as you make your way through the twistings and turnings of the maze to the center, where you will find the Minotaur." Then she handed Theseus his sword. "Once you have killed the monster with your sword, you can follow the trail of thread back out to the entrance of the Labyrinth."

The next day, when the time came for the Athenian victims to enter the Labyrinth, Theseus, as befitted a hero and a prince, volunteered to go first. He hid the sword and ball of thread so that the Cretans could not see them. Just inside the entrance to the maze, he made fast one end of the thread, just as he had planned to do. He unwound the thread as he traveled this way and that through the passageways. He was dazed by the turnings in the maze, for at times the corners changed so abruptly that Theseus could not see three steps in front of him.

Finally, Theseus entered a wide hall in the center of the Labyrinth and came face to face with the Minotaur. The dreaded monster reared up on its muscular hind legs and tossed its horns from side to side, slobbering from its thick lips. The beast roared and charged at Theseus, tossing the hero to the floor. But Theseus thrust upward with his trusty sword and the Minotaur clambered off Theseus, screaming in pain. As Theseus

gazed at the monster, he thought of all the young Athenians that the creature had eaten. Anger filled the breast of the hero, and he charged the Minotaur, running through him again with his sword. The beast shuddered and died, and Theseus, exhausted but triumphant, left his sword in the Minotaur's neck.

Theseus then found the end of the thread and followed it back to the entrance of the Labyrinth, where the other Athenians waited with Ariadne. They hugged him in relief and happiness at their escape from the dreaded Minotaur. Ariadne was also filled with joy at Theseus' success, but she knew that she could no longer stay in her father's palace, because she had betrayed him by helping Theseus.

Theseus led the young Athenians and Ariadne to their black-sailed ship. They sailed to Naxos, an island in the Aegean Sea in southeastern Greece. Some storytellers say that Theseus left Ariadne on the island while she was sleeping and that Dionysus, god of wine, music, and dancing, rescued her. Others say Theseus decided to abandon her, because he had become ashamed of her betrayal of her father. Still others say she became seasick, so Theseus put her ashore while he worked on chores on the ship. Unfortunately, a terrible storm arose and blew the ship away. By the time Theseus returned, Ariadne was dead. In any case, Theseus deserted Ariadne.

All versions of the story agree that Theseus forgot to change the ship's sails from black to white. When Aegeus saw the black sails, he jumped off a rocky cliff into the sea and died. Thereafter, the sea was known as the Aegean Sea, the name by which it is still known today.

After Aegeus died, Theseus became king of Athens. Legend has it that he brought democracy to Greece by uniting many villages in Attica, the region where Athens was located. He went on to have many other adventures. Because of his heroic deeds, Theseus achieved his goal of becoming a great hero, and the Greeks often compared him to the great hero Heracles.

QUESTIONS AND ANSWERS

Q: *Before King Aegeus returned from Troezen to Athens, he hid two objects under a large stone. What were they, what was Theseus to do with them, and what did these objects symbolize?*

A: Aegeus hid a sword and a pair of sandals under a large rock. If Theseus could roll away this stone, he was to bring the sword and sandals to Athens, where Aegeus would recognize him as his son and heir. The sword and sandals represented Theseus' noble lineage and heroic qualities.

Q: *On the road between Troezen and Athens, Theseus conquered six menaces, including monsters, bandits, and robbers. What were they and by what means did he defeat each one?*

A: Theseus smashed the skull of the bandit Periphetes, the "Clubber," using Periphetes' own club. He tied the robber Sinis to two bent pine trees so that they would spring forward and tear him in half. Theseus then forced the bandit Sciron to wash his feet, and when Sciron bent to do so, Theseus kickd him into the sea. With his spear and sword, Theseus killed the Sow of Crommyon. He crushed Cercyon to death in a wrestling match. Finally, Theseus killed Procrustes, the "Stretcher," using the same bed that Procrustes used to kill his victims.

Q: *What did Theseus do to the Bull of Marathon?*

A: Theseus captured the bull and brought it to Athens, where he gave it to Aegeus, who sacrificed the bull to the god Apollo.

Q: *What was the tribute Athens had to pay to King Minos of Crete and why?*

A: Athenians had killed the son of King Minos when he was visiting Athens. Every nine years after that, Minos demanded that Athens send seven young men and seven young women to be sacrificed to the Minotaur, a half-bull, half-man monster.

Q: *What was the Labyrinth and how is this term used today?*

A: It was a complex maze designed by Daedalus, an inventor from Crete. Today, any complex maze is called a labyrinth. The term is also applied to a garden maze formed by paths separated by high hedges or to any situation that is particularly complex.

Q: *Theseus sailed from Athens with black sails on his ship to indicate the city's sadness at having to send its young people as tribute to Minos. What was Theseus supposed to do with these sails if he killed the Minotaur? What did he do instead and what was the result?*

A: Theseus was supposed to change the sails to white to indicate to his father from afar that Theseus had killed the Minotaur. Theseus forgot to change the sails. When his father, Aegeus, saw that the sails were still black, he thought Theseus was dead. Aegeus then threw himself off a rocky cliff into the sea and died. To this day, the sea is known as the Aegean Sea.

EXPERT COMMENTARY

Of all the heroes of Greek mythology, Theseus is the one most likely to have been a real person. Joseph Campbell, noted mythological scholar, wrote: "Theseus, the hero-slayer of the Minotaur, entered Crete from without, as the symbol and arm of the rising civilization of the Greeks."[5] Theseus became an important political symbol in the fifth century B.C. in Athens. According to Lucilla Burn, the curator of the department of Greek and Roman antiquities at the British Museum:

> Theseus was the quintessential Athenian hero, the embodiment of all the Athenians thought was the best and most distinctive about themselves. He was endowed with most of the superhuman characteristics as Herakles [sic], and his deeds were almost as impressive. But he was more refined and civilised than Herakles [sic], a consummate statesman who could number among his achievements not merely the establishment of such religious and social institutions as the great Panathenaic festival of Athens, but also the political consolidation of Attica and the foundation of the Athenian democracy.[6]

In 476–475 B.C., Athenian political leader Cimon found the bones of a very large man, a bronze spearhead, and a sword on Scyros, an island east of Attica, where Theseus was reputed to have died. Cimon brought these relics to Athens, where they were reburied in a shrine in the center of the city which honored Theseus.

Even in ancient times, scholars tried to differentiate between historical truth and myth in stories about Crete. Classics professor Barry B. Powell considered historian Thucydides (460?–400 B.C.) a pioneer in efforts to distinguish myth from history. Powell noted: "In the fifth century B.C., the Athenian writer Thucydides, in the introduction to his history of the

Peloponnesian War, argued from mythic accounts that the kingdom of Minos was the first *thalassocracy*, a political order having 'supremacy over the sea.'"[7] Here are comments about Minos in Thucydides' own words, translated from the Greek:

> Minos was the first whom we know–granted, only by hearsay—to build a navy. He was able to take control of most of the Aegean Sea, to govern the islands we call the Cyclades, and to start colonies in many of them. First of all, he had to drive out the Carians. (A people of Asia Minor.) He then set up his own sons as rulers, and, as far as he could, wiped out the pirates, no doubt in the hope that their income would thereafter flow into his own pockets.[8]

Archaeological excavation has provided evidence of the existence of the palace and Labyrinth of King Minos. Professor Powell explained:

> The archaeological record behind myths about Crete lay buried until 1899 when Englishman Arthur Evans . . . purchased with his own funds part of the north-central plain of Crete, where a low mound showed promise of concealing ancient remains. There he gradually uncovered the ruins of ancient Cnossus, an enormous palace complex dating from the earliest European civilization, which flourished from about 3100 B.C. to about 1000 B.C. . . . It was Evans who applied the term *Minoan* (after the legendary Minos) to this culture and to the people who fashioned it. Since Evans's day, archaeologists have enlarged his excavations at Cnossus and explored many other palace sites on Crete.[9]

Glossary

aegis—A breastplate, or shield, worn for protection in battle.

archaeology—The study of ancient cultures.

arete—The ancient Greek concept of striving for excellence, a particular goal of heroes.

bile—Venomous liquid inside a body cavity.

castanets—A type of rattle.

cauldron—A large pot.

centaur—A creature with a human head and chest, and the legs and body of a horse.

fate—The belief that life's outcomes are predetermined by the gods.

Gorgon—One of three sisters known for turning anyone or anything that looked at them to stone.

helmsman—The crew member who steers a ship.

hero cults—A system of religious beliefs and practices in honor of a particular hero.

hubris—Excessive pride, a characteristic often demonstrated by Greek heroes.

kibisis—The magical pouch that Theseus used to carry the head of the Gorgon Medusa; it always became exactly the right size to accommodate whatever was carried in it.

labor—A task requiring great physical or mental strength.

lair—An animal's hiding place.

lyre—A stringed instrument.

nymphs—Divine spirits that lived in various habitats such as trees, lakes, and streams. They were often depicted as young women.

oracle—A priest or priestess through whom a particular god was thought to speak; also refers to the shrine of this priest and the prophecies that the priest gave.

pantheon—The group or collection of Greek gods and goddesses.

prow—The pointed front of a ship.

pyre—A bed of materials that are formed into a tall pile onto which a body is placed and burned at a funeral.

quiver—A cylindrical arrow holder that has a long strap for holding it over the shoulder.

scimitar—A small, sharp, curved sword.

shades—Ghosts of the dead.

sorceress—A witch.

spring—A well or water source gushing up from the ground.

squire—A manservant.

stadium—A large, enclosed, oval athletic field.

staff—A tall pole.

stern—The rear of a ship.

strait—A waterway joining two other bodies of water.

thalassocracy—A political order having supremacy over the sea.

tribute—A payment from one ruler to another to acknowledge submission.

usurp—To steal or take away an individual's rightful possession, as in usurping a throne.

Chapter Notes

Preface

1. Mark P. O. Morford and Robert J. Lenardon, *Classical Mythology*, 6th ed. (New York: Longman, Addison-Wesley Educational Publishers Inc., 1999), p. 1.

2. Michael Grant, *Myths of the Greeks and Romans* (New York: Meridian, 1995), p. 28.

3. Bernard Knox, "Introduction," in Robert Fagles, trans., *Homer: The Iliad* (New York: Penguin Books, 1990), pp. 5–6.

4. Henry J. Walker, *Theseus and Athens* (New York: Oxford University Press, 1995), p. 6.

5. Ibid., p. 5.

6. Barry B. Powell, *Classical Myth*, 2nd ed. (Upper Saddle River, N.J.: Prentice Hall, 1998), p. 7.

7. Ibid.

8. Peter R. Stillman, *Introduction to Myth* (Portsmouth, N.H.: Boynton/Cook Publishers, 1985), pp. 35-85, and Reg Harris and Susan Thompson, *The Hero's Journey: A Guide to Literature and Life* (Napa, Calif.: Ariane Publications, 1997), p. 25.

9. Stillman, p. 33.

Chapter 1. Perseus and the Gorgon Medusa

1. Edith Hamilton, *Mythology* (New York: Warner Books, 1999), p. 146.

2. Barry B. Powell, *Classical Myth*, 2nd ed. (Upper Saddle River, N.J.: Prentice Hall, 1998), p. 389.

3. Kevin Osborn and Dana L. Burgess, *The Complete Idiot's Guide to Classical Mythology* (New York: Alpha Books, 1998), p. 117.

Chapter 2. Atalanta

1. Barry B. Powell, *Classical Myth*, 2nd ed. (Upper Saddle River, N.J.: Prentice Hall, 1998), p. 36.

2. Ibid.

3. Ibid.

4. Michael Grant, *Myths of the Greeks and Romans* (New York: Meridian, 1995), p. 345.

5. Ibid., pp. 344–345.

6. Edith Hamilton, *Mythology* (New York: Warner Books, 1999), p. 180.

7. Martin P. Nilsson, *Greek Folk Religion* (Philadelphia, Penn.: University of Pennsylvania Press, 1998), p. 96.

Chapter 3. The Calydonian Boar Hunt

1. Donna Rosenberg and Sorelle Baker, *Mythology and You* (Lincolnwood, Ill.: National Textbook Company, p. 1992), p. 176.

2. Robert Graves, *The Greek Myths*, combined ed. (London, England: Penguin Books, 1992), note 1, p. 267.

3. Mark P.O. Morford and Robert J. Lenardon, *Classical Mythology*, 6th ed. (New York: Longman, Addison-Wesley Educational Publishers Inc., 1999), p. 84.

4. Ibid., note 21, p. 603.

5. Rosenberg and Baker, note 3, p. 184.

Chapter 4. Jason and the Argonauts

1. Lucilla Burn, *Greek Myths* (Austin, Tex.: University of Texas Press, 1990), p. 59.

2. Apollonios Rhodios, *The Argonautika*, trans. Peter Green (Berkeley, Calif.: University of Berkeley Press, 1997), p. 40.

3. Mark P.O. Morford and Robert J. Lenardon, *Classical Mythology*, 6th ed. (New York: Longman, Addison-Wesley Educational Publishers Inc., 1999), p. 464.

4. Rhodios, p. 39.

5. Joseph Campbell, *The Hero with a Thousand Faces* (Princeton, N.J.: Princeton University Press, 1973), pp. 197–198.

6. Ibid., pp. 203–204.

7. Edith Hamilton, Mythology (New York: Time Warner Books, 1999), p. 122.

8. Michael Grant, *Myths of the Greeks and Romans* (New York: Meridian, 1995), p. 259.

9. Rhodios, back cover.

Chapter 5. The Labors of Heracles

1. Edith Hamilton, *Mythology* (New York: Time Warner Books, 1999), pp. 166–167

2. Lucilla Burn, *Greek Myths* (Austin, Tex.: University of Texas Press, 1990), p. 24.

3. Ibid., p. 16.

4. Mark P.O. Morford and Robert J. Lenardon, *Classical Mythology*, 6th ed. (New York: Longman, Addison-Wesley Educational Publishers Inc., 1999), p. 434.

5. Barry B. Powell, *Classical Myth*, 2nd ed. (Upper Saddle River, N.J.: Prentice Hall, 1998), p. 396.

6. Morford and Lenardon, p. 435.

Chapter 6. The Lernaean Hydra and the Death of Heracles

1. Mark P.O. Morford and Robert J. Lenardon, *Classical Mythology*, 6th ed. (New York: Longman, Addison-Wesley Educational Publishers Inc., 1999), p. 420.

2. Barry B. Powell, *Classical Myth*, 2nd ed. (Upper Saddle River, N.J.: Prentice Hall, 1998), p. 426.

3. Pindar, "Texts and Translations," *Isthmian Odes*, n.d. <www.perseus.tufts.edu> (March, 2001).

Chapter 7. Theseus and the Minotaur

1. Internet source: Commentary on Chapter 21 of Classical Mythology, http://longman.awl.com/mythology/chaptertopics/commentary_21.asp.

2. Ibid.

3. Lucilla Burn, *Greek Myths* (Austin, Tex.: University of Texas Press, 1990), p. 25.

4. Ibid., p. 27.

5. Joseph Campbell, *The Hero with a Thousand Faces*, 2nd ed. (Princeton, N.J.: Princeton University Press, 1968), p. 17.

6. Burn, p. 25.

7. Barry B. Powell, *Classical Myth*, 2nd ed. (Upper Saddle River, N.J.: Prentice Hall, 1998), p. 367.

8. Ibid.

9. Ibid.

Further Reading

Balit, Christina and Jo Napoli Donna. *Treasury of Greek Mythology: Classic Stories of Gods, Goddesses and Heroes & Monsters.* California: National Geographic Children's Books, 2011.

Green, Lancelyn Charles. *Tales of the Greek Heroes.* New York: Penguin Group, 2009.

Kingsley, Charles. *Heroes of Greek Mythology.* Massachusettes: Digireads.com, 2009.

Internet Addresses

Gods and Heroes

<http://www.mythweb.com>

Encyclopedia Mythica: Greek mythology

<http://www.pantheon.org/areas/mythology/
europe/greek/>

ABC Arts Online: Winged Sandals

<http://www.abc.net.au/arts/wingedsandals/>

Index

7/26/12.

31.93